derek acorah's
AMAZING pSYCHiC STORIEs

derek
acorah's
AMAZING
pSYCHIC
STORIEs

Derek Acorah

HarperElement
An Imprint of HarperCollins*Publishers*
77–85 Fulham Palace Road
Hammersmith, London W6 8JB

The website address is: www.thorsonselement.com

and *HarperElement* are trademarks of
HarperCollins*Publishers* Limited

First published by HarperElement 2006

© Derek Acorah 2006

Derek Acorah asserts the moral right to
be identified as the author of this work

A catalogue record for this book is
available from the British Library

ISBN-13 978-0-00-722066-3
ISBN-10 0-00-722066-9

Printed and bound in Great Britain by
Clays Ltd, St Ives plc

This book is proudly printed on paper which contains wood
from well managed forests, certified in accordance with the
rules of the Forest Stewardship Council. For more information
about FSC, please visit www.fsc.org

Mixed Sources
Product group from well-managed
forests and other controlled sources
www.fsc.org Cert no. SW-COC-1806
© 1996 Forest Stewardship Council

Dedicated to the memory of Bill and Joanie

Contents

Acknowledgements

I would like first to thank all the people who have helped in the writing of this book by sharing their experiences with me.

I am indebted as ever to my wife, Gwen, and to my agent, Stuart Hobday, who have both been stalwarts in their support of me over the past year. I am also indebted to my family and all the other people who have stood by me and believed in me in spite of everything.

I am especially indebted to Ray Rodaway, who is my tour manager but more importantly my friend. Ray has been by my side throughout my travels around the country whilst I have been conducting my theatre demonstrations and also filming *Derek Acorah's Ghost Towns*. Life would have been very much more difficult during these times if it had not been for the presence of 'Rodders'.

Recently I have been through some interesting times. Some things have happened which should not have happened but were perhaps meant in order to test my dedication to my work for spirit. Other things have happened which have brought me much happiness and enjoyment, such as the creation by Richard Woolfe, then of LIVINGtv, of the television programme *Derek Acorah's Ghost Towns*. I have enjoyed every moment of the filming of this programme and have to extend my heartfelt thanks to the production crew and especially to Danniella Westbrook and Angus Purden for making this so.

I feel that I have come through these 'testing' times with a great deal more strength of character than I previously possessed and I am looking forward to the future with excitement.

Introduction

My name is Derek Acorah. I am a spirit medium. I have been working professionally as a medium for over 25 years now. During the course of my work I have come across many, many instances where divine intervention has taken place – those occasions when we just know that somebody up there is looking after us.

We all have our own different ideas about the workers in the world beyond – those who are charged with the task of guiding our footsteps through this earthly life, those who care for us and prevent us from making errors of judgement or foolhardy decisions that would cause us to undergo experiences not meant for us in this lifetime. Some people refer to these astral beings as their 'guardian angels'. Others, like myself, refer to them as 'spirit guides' and 'helpers' or 'guardians'.

However we think of these beings, we all have guiding influences in the heavenly realms who have been allocated to us from birth and who will remain with us for as long as we live on this Earth plane. We may not be aware of their presence, and indeed, some would say that there is no such thing, but I can promise you that there is. You may not be able to see them or hear them, but I doubt that there is anybody alive in this world today who has not at some time or other been inspired by spirit to make a decision which has altered their life quite radically in some way. It may be a last-minute change of plan that has resulted in the avoidance of an accident; it may be going somewhere on the spur of the moment and meeting a person who has changed everything. Such events don't take place randomly – they are meant to happen. They are engineered by our guides so that we can experience just what we are meant to in order to fulfil the decisions regarding lifetime experiences that we ourselves made before incarnating into this life.

As well as spirit guides, there are of course the true angels – those celestial beings who draw close to us in moments of great stress or loss, or even as a sign of something momentous that is about to take place in our life. These angels are not human beings returned from the spirit world – they have never incarnated into this world in human form. They are pure positive energies in much the same manner as poltergeists, which are pure negative energies. Neither angels nor poltergeists have ever taken human form in an earthly life.

The Celestial Caretakers' Spiritual Hierarchy

In every society there is a hierarchy and the people at the top have worked hard in order to earn their position. The world of spirit is no different.

When a person leaves their physical life and returns home to the heavenly state they enter a period of recuperation. Once they are ready to take their rightful place once more in the spirit world they are asked what they feel they have achieved during their incarnation here on Earth and whether they feel that they have learned the lessons necessary for their soul's growth.

What, you may ask, is the point of 'soul growth'? The more a spirit experiences during its physical lifetimes, then the more it grows and progresses. The ultimate aim is to achieve a position as a teacher or main guide, helping someone through their physical life.

Beyond the status of 'guide' lies the pathway towards the spiritual hierarchy – the 'Old Ones', as I like to refer to them. The Old Ones are those spirits who no longer return to the earthly environs. They inhabit the highest celestial realms. They have experienced everything, they have no more learning to undergo, they have evolved completely. They are as near to perfection as it is possible for any spirit to be and are closest to our creator God.

The Old Ones are the spirit masters who speak to the spirit masses in the Great Halls of Understanding. They teach them about what is expected of them and talk to them about what they have learned in their earthly incarnations and what they feel they ought to learn in their next physical lives on Earth.

The Old Ones also have the responsibility of monitoring those people who have been elected leaders of our physical world – the heads of state, prime ministers and others who have been charged with the well-being of the people. It is the Old Ones who step in and alter the course of history when they consider that it is necessary for the greater good of mankind.

It is also the Old Ones who are responsible for the laws of karma. They have to ensure that every karmic debt, whether positive or negative, is repaid in full.

Below the Old Ones come the 'Caretakers'. These spirits are not quite so highly evolved as the Old Ones but are sufficiently experienced to act as guardians and spirit guides to people in their physical lives. They also have the opportunity to reincarnate into a physical life themselves once or twice more to undergo more of life's experiences, should they so wish, in order to achieve the ultimate Old One status.

During a final incarnation, I believe that the Caretakers have a particular duty: to try to help us reorder the way our lives are lived so that our Earth becomes a more heavenly place. I believe that people such as Jesus Christ, Buddha and Mohammed decided that before taking their place in the highest celestial realms they would return to a physical incarnation one last time in order to help humanity.

The Caretakers look after all the realms of spirit. The more highly evolved a Caretaker, the higher the realm of spirit that they are responsible for. The Caretakers with more to learn consequently oversee the realms of the younger spirits and the spirit people with more to learn.

The Caretakers are therefore responsible for newly discarnate spirits entering the spirit realms. They make sure that everything is ready for their entry into the state of rest and recuperation once they have been delivered by their spirit guide and their family members from their physical lifetime. After spirits have successfully recuperated, Caretakers will help them to review that lifetime and to determine whether they feel that they have achieved what they intended to achieve or not. Discussion will also take place with regard to the spirit's next incarnation, what it hopes to achieve and whether that lifetime's experience should be easier or harsher than the last incarnation. Ultimately the decision as to what will be experienced in a physical lifetime and when reincarnation will take place is entirely up to the spirit. It may decide to reincarnate almost immediately or may wait aeons before taking up the challenge of yet another physical incarnation.

Each of us has made these choices. They are ours alone, but throughout each incarnation we are guided along life's pathway. Guardian angels, spirit guides and family members in spirit can all make their presence felt in our lives, both to help us keep to our chosen life's experience and to encourage us when the going gets tough. Many, many people have had such experiences and I am happy to be able to tell their stories here.

Chapter 1

My Meetings with Angels

So far in my lifetime I have experienced being in the company of a true angel twice. The first time was when I visited California in 1998.

On the day prior to my return to the United Kingdom I was sitting in a diner in Marina del Rey in the company of some members of the International Society for Paranormal Research, including Dr Larry Montz. Quite out of the blue I became aware of a presence with me. Feelings of absolute joy, divine delight and pure love flooded through my being. I had never felt anything like it before. I was moved to tears by the sheer force of emotion. I felt changed and enlightened. I knew that the experience had been brought to me to help me understand my mission in life to tell the whole world the truth of eternal life.

The second occasion I experienced a meeting with a true angel was in the back garden of my home. My father Fred had passed on to the spirit world the previous November and I knew that the time was drawing near for my beloved dog Cara to pass on to the world of spirit as well. I was deeply saddened. Cara had been my trusted companion for almost 17 years and in all of those years she had never left my side. She had been with me during some very bad times and had shared the good times with me too. She was 'my girl' and I did not know how I was going to cope without her loving physical presence.

As I sat with my head in my hands contemplating what was shortly to take place, I heard a gentle rustling noise. A feeling of warmth, peace and all-encompassing love flooded through my whole body just like the feelings I had experienced that afternoon in Marina del Rey. I was enveloped in dazzling pure white light and once again I cried with the pure loving emotion of the experience. My deep sadness was replaced by a complete calmness and acceptance of what was to be. As the light evaporated and the celestial being withdrew from me, I knew that my Cara would be safe in her heavenly home and that my father would care for her until we were once more reunited.

It is interesting to note that the circumstances surrounding me at these times were entirely different. On the first occasion I was in the company of other people and the atmosphere was positive and upbeat. There had been animated conversation about a bright future. It seemed to be something within that conversation that caused the angelic visitation. It was as though the heavenly realms were setting their seal upon it. As Dr Larry Montz said, 'I think that today we have been visited by this spirit for a specific reason – to tell us we are walking on our predestined pathway.'

On the second occasion when I felt an angelic presence I could not have been feeling less positive. I knew that my beloved dog's health was failing fast and I was at the point where I had to make the ultimate decision regarding having her euthanased. I cannot describe how I felt. I loved Cara dearly and could not bear to let her go. But if I loved her, I asked myself, how could I let her continue to deteriorate to the point where life for her would be painful and difficult? It was the most awful decision I have ever had to make in my life and it was then that the angel visited me. On that occasion I feel it was to bring me peace and let me know that the correct thing for Cara had to be done. It was to remind me that she would pass over peacefully knowing that she was loved and that I loved her enough to let her go on to the beautiful place waiting for her. It was to remind me that she would not be alone – that my father Fred would take care of her until it was time for us to be reunited in spirit. It was to give me solace at a time when I was very, very sad indeed.

Whatever the circumstances, when you are visited by a true celestial being the feelings of peace and love are so intense. Warmth radiates to both the inner and the outer self. I can only describe it as a 'living light'.

It is curious that it is only relatively recently that people have begun to speak of their experiences with true angels. This may be because in the past such stories have been dismissed as claptrap and silliness. But angels exist just as surely as you and I.

When a person is truly blessed by an angelic visitation, their descriptions are always the same – an awareness that the light around them has become dazzlingly bright and an atmosphere of intense peace, love and happiness. As the angelic presence recedes, it leaves behind positive feelings. Visitation from an angel is a truly life-changing experience.

People see true angels at different times and for different reasons. The most common reason for angelic visitation is to give strength to a person who is feeling sad or lost, to give them hope for better in the future. Other people experience angelic visitation when they are ill. People also see angels at times of great happiness and report that seeing the angel is an affirmation of that happiness. In short, angels can be anywhere at any time and in any circumstances.

An angel visited Penny when she moved home as a six-year-old child. She was with her parents and her brother but was somewhat afraid of the house that the family was to move into.

As Penny nervously entered the bedroom that was to be hers, she noticed a very bright light in the corner of the room. As she stared at the light she began to see the outline of what she described as 'the sort of angel you see in picture books'.

From that point onwards Penny wasn't afraid of her room. She felt happy and peaceful there and spent many happy childhood years in the house.

And so an angel came to make a nervous little girl feel happy and at peace at a time when her life was changing.

CHAPTER 2

White Feathers

When people describe angelic visitation, it is not uncommon for them to report the mysterious appearance of a white feather. This is meant to let you know that an angel has been around in your time of need or that you are not forgotten and that life goes on.

There have been occasions when an inexplicable white feather has been discovered in my own home. We do not have any caged birds as pets and although there is a garden frequented by many birds, none have ever been inadvertently trapped in the house. The feathers have always been discovered lying on a kitchen worktop and never in the bedrooms or anywhere on the upper floors where it would be possible for a feather to escape from bedding. Our cats have never brought a dead bird into the house, so that explanation is out of the question too. I have even seen a feather drifting down from the ceiling and gently landing on the kitchen work surface. There is no explanation whatsoever for the appearance of such feathers in our home. It can only be the work of an angel.

Angels are of course everywhere, and everybody, whether they recognize the fact or not, will at some time have their life touched by an angelic being. Not all angelic visitation is of the celestial nature – we can also be visited by our 'guardian angels', those people who have once taken human form and who care for us from the world beyond.

A white feather may be dismissed as insignificant or not even noticed. There are some people, though, who set great store by a white feather featuring in their life.

One such person is a young woman whose son passed to the world of spirit at a very young age due to a serious illness. On the anniversary of his passing and at other times during the year when she is feeling particularly low, she will always find a white feather. There is never an explanation as to why the feathers should be found where they are, but they give the young woman comfort and, she feels, the knowledge that her son is always around her and draws even closer when he feels his mother needs uplifting.

Another woman who has found white feathers is Carole. Although I have not met her, she has kindly allowed me to tell you about her tragic experience.

Carole's husband passed to spirit very suddenly at the age of 47 as the result of a massive heart attack. Tragically, this awful event took place whilst Carole was out of the house and her husband was in the company of their two teenage children. As you can imagine, it was a terrible time for the small family, but gradually they began to get back some sort of normality and were coping well.

Carole firmly believes that her husband is her guardian angel and I have to agree. From what she tells me, he is guiding and guarding his family just as much as he ever did whilst he was here in his physical life. Carole tells me that whenever she has to take on a task that her husband would have performed in the past, such as checking the oil in the car or fixing something in the house, she sees a white feather somewhere in her path. She has grown to expect them now and is never disappointed!

In her quiet times Carole often reflects on days gone by. She tells me that on such occasions she feels her husband's presence strongly, even to the point of feeling a slight pressure on her shoulder or her hand being gently held – proof indeed that her husband has not gone away but is there as much as he ever was and no doubt always will be.

So the symbolic white feather brings huge comfort to a bereaved wife, confirming to her that her husband is safe and well and still caring for her from the world beyond.

Rebecca is also been the recipient of white feathers.

Rebecca suffered serious depression after a horrendous and almost fatal attack by an ex-boyfriend of her mother's. Whilst still on medication for her depression she went out with her friends one night. She was unaware that taking an alcoholic drink would affect the medication she had been prescribed and returned home even more depressed and upset than ever. She attempted to commit suicide but fortunately was found in time and taken to hospital, where she stayed overnight.

When she arrived home, she went straight to bed. The windows and door to her bedroom were tightly shut. After a long sleep Rebecca awoke to find a large white feather on her bed. She is convinced that it was from her grand-father in spirit, who also suffered terribly with depres-sion, and that he had come to give her comfort and tell her that everything would be alright.

Since that incident Rebecca tells me that she has been finding white feathers every now and again in some very strange places. I have to agree that it is very likely that her grandfather is in visitation. He is letting her know that he understands what she is going through and is watching over her.

Maureen inherited a small dog named Leckie after her cousin and his wife sadly passed on to the spirit world within 18 months of one another.

A year or so after taking Leckie into her home, Maureen began to suffer with arthritis that was sometimes so severe that she was unable to walk. Happily, the little dog was there to comfort and amuse her and keep her company. On really bad days he would cuddle up close to Maureen as if he was comforting her.

Sadly, in time Leckie too passed on to the spirit world. Maureen was very upset at losing him and felt an unreasonable anger at her cousin for leaving him with her in the first place. She felt so bitter and angry that she had lost her cousin, his wife and little Leckie that she went along to her cousin's grave and removed the dog's photograph that she had placed there three months earlier.

The following morning Maureen found the most beautiful soft white feather lying next to her sofa. It was in the exact spot where Leckie used to lie and sleep. Maureen wondered whether it was a calling card from an angel to help her through her grieving period or whether it was from Leckie himself to reassure her that he was still close by when she was lying alone and suffering with her arthritis.

Since that day Maureen's anger and bitterness at losing her family members has left her. The love that she always had for them has been restored. That little doggie angel's work has been done!

Wanda was holidaying with her family in a sixteenth-century cottage in Cornwall. She felt very uneasy after the first day or so and was sure it was haunted. Because she knew that she had almost two weeks left of her holiday she decided that she would pray to the angels for protection for her family from whatever was in the cottage.

The next day her sister reported that she had seen a figure with huge wings walking past the front window. She was convinced it was an angel and added that it had left a large white feather.

Wanda's partner was not convinced and said that if angels existed, could they leave a sign, such as another feather. Moments later Wanda's son rushed to where his parents were sitting. 'Mum, a huge white feather has just dropped down from the ceiling in the living room!' he shouted.

Wanda thought he had probably been listening to the conversation and told him, 'Yeah, sure it did!', but he was insistent.

Wanda's sister went to collect the feather that she had found earlier and Wanda's son produced his feather. They were both pure white! Was it a coincidence? We will never know. What is known, though, is that Wanda was not bothered for the rest of her holiday by the ghostly resident of the cottage.

Lois is also convinced that she has experienced angelic visitation.

Lois tells me that in the early spring of 2005 she was at her workplace. The radio was playing in the background and she got up to change the station. She tuned in to a programme that featured an interview with me. At the end I described my experience with the angel who brought me such peace and comfort just prior to the passing of my beloved dog Cara.

Afterwards Lois walked over to the window and as she stood there looking out and thinking about the story of the angel, what appeared to be a feather floated down from the sky and landed gracefully on the ground right in front of her. Thinking it was her imagination, she rushed downstairs and ran outside to where the feather had landed. She was amazed to see that there on the ground lay a beautiful white feather. She picked it up and brought it inside.

Later that evening Lois showed her husband the feather and told him about the radio interview. She says that she did feel a little stupid and thought that she might be reading a little too much into the arrival of the feather, as it could well have been a coincidence that a bird's feather had fallen whilst she was thinking about angels. She says that her husband Craig may have felt that too.

The following week Lois and Craig travelled to America. On the day that they were leaving to travel back to the UK, as they were loading up the car with luggage, a large white feather blew into the hallway, stopping at their feet.

Two weeks after returning to the UK Lois' father passed on to the spirit world. She was devastated. There have also been a number of other events that have caused her concern, not least the danger of losing her sight due to her diabetic condition However, she writes that things are starting to get much better in all areas, including her eyesight. She says:

'Although I have never told my friends or family about the feathers, as they'd most probably think I was oversensitive and losing the plot a bit, I firmly believe that the significance of the feathers in my life was to let me know I wasn't alone and to give me strength for the tough times that were to come, to comfort me with the knowledge that my dad hasn't left me and is being looked after in spirit. The feathers did not protect me from or stop any of the pain and difficulties that were to enter my life, but I am sure my ability to cope would have been much less without them. I believe that my feeling that the angels had given me a sign made me think about things more spiritually and allowed me to put my difficulties much more in perspective in relation to the bigger picture of human existence. All of us have difficult times in our lives, some more so than others, but I feel it is how we choose to deal with the difficulties that teaches us the lessons we need to learn. For this I am eternally grateful to the angels for their interaction in my life.'

I could not have put it better myself!

Of course the arrival of a white feather is not necessarily a sign that there is an angel around. I recall sitting in the passenger seat of my vehicle one day whilst Ray Rodaway, my tour manager, was driving me to a theatre venue in the south of England. We had been travelling for a couple of hours or more and had decided to stop at a motorway service station. It was a very cold day so we both put on our jackets prior to leaving the vehicle.

We returned to the car approximately half an hour later and took to the road once more. We had been travelling for no more than a few minutes when I heard Ray say, 'Aye, Ackers! You know what you were saying about angels – when there's one about you sometimes see a white feather?'

I nodded.

'Well,' Ray continued, 'I think there must be one about now because a white feather's just drifted down from the roof of the car. You don't think we're being warned that we're about to have an accident, do you?'

I looked at Ray sharply but could see from his expression that he was really very serious. In fact he looked rather nervous. And sure enough, when I looked at the dashboard of the car, there sat a small white feather.

As I looked in Ray's direction again I could see a small pinprick of white sticking through the outer material of his jacket. I pulled it and out popped a small white feather.

'No, Ray,' I said dryly, 'there aren't any angels around just now. The only feathers being shed at the moment are by you and your duvet jacket!'

An expression of relief spread across Ray's face, followed quickly by one of embarrassment. 'Don't tell anybody about it, will you, Ackers?' he said.

By this time I was convulsed with laughter. 'Oh, Rods! This one is too good *not* to share!'

CHAPTER 3

Following Our Destiny

Guardian angels, spirit guides and family members in spirit do not of course reserve the right to make their presence felt in our lives only when we are in mortal danger or when we need reassurance. Our guides and guardians are designated to us at birth to ensure that we conduct our lives in the manner chosen by us prior to our incarnation into this physical life. Because we have free will, our God-given right, we may put ourselves in danger of choosing the wrong pathway and veering away from our chosen life's experience, and it is the job of our guardians and guides to make sure that we do not stray.

My own life is the perfect example of somebody who started off on one pathway only to be forced some years later to meet my destiny – just as my grandmother had foretold many years previously.

The one aim in my life when I was a child was to become a professional footballer. If anybody asked me what I was going to do when I grew up, my answer would always be: 'Play football for Liverpool!' If pressed to consider another possibility, I might reluctantly say that being a train driver might be interesting, but I never seriously considered it. I had my heart set on playing football.

Throughout my childhood I experienced proof of the existence of a spirit world and I had been told by my grandmother that I would follow in her footsteps and work for spirit by one day becoming a medium. However, I had proclaimed that I didn't want to 'be a gook' and privately had pooh-poohed the idea. I did not question that there was a world beyond and that people came from that world into our world and mingled with us just as they had when they were in their physical lives – I had received more than enough proof of that – but I did not want to work with those spirit people. I wanted to be a footballer!

Finally my ambitions were fulfilled – I was signed at 15 years of age as an apprentice professional footballer with Liverpool Football Club. Gleefully I would tell my mother, 'Gran was wrong! Look! I'm a footballer!'

What I did not know at that time was that although my ambition was being fulfilled, my ultimate destiny would still have to be met. Before incarnating into this physical life I had made a promise and that promise had to be kept.

I was allowed a certain amount of success as a footballer, but did not achieve the standard that I wished. My footballing career came to an end at a relatively early age and I was left with no choice but to follow the pathway that was meant for me – the pathway that I myself had chosen whilst still resident in the world of spirit prior to my incarnation here. As my grandmother had foreseen and as I myself had promised, I would become a worker for spirit – a medium – and a medium I became! It was my destiny!

I had reason to be talking to a young man in his thirties one day. I will respect his wish to remain anonymous and will merely call him 'David'. His story is one where spirit, rather than working in mysterious ways, brought this young man to the realization that he was on the wrong pathway rather abruptly.

David's story began in one of the poorer areas of Liverpool. He was the youngest of three brothers in a family which was not very well off at all. In fact most of the time money was very tight indeed. David's mother and father both worked when there was work available and consequently were away from the family home most of the day. David and his brothers were left to a great extent to fend for themselves. Boys will be boys, and in their harsh environment it was not long before David was playing truant. Time went by and his appearances at school became less and less frequent. By the time David was 14 years of age he rarely attended school at all. He was a tall well-built lad who appeared older than he was, and eventually he became part of a group of teenagers who were known as 'no goods' in the area. If ever there was trouble David would be there in the thick of things. Stealing cars and joy-riding were activities that took place on a weekly basis. David thought there was nothing like the excitement of stealing a car with his mates and driving to Southport at high speed. On one such occasion the car he was in careered off the road and ended up in a field. David and his friend were badly cut and bruised – they were fortunate to escape with their lives.

By the time David was 15 he was well known to the local police and had been in court on numerous occasions. The day eventually arrived when he was sent away to a correctional institution for a number of months. When he was released he merely picked up his old lifestyle, but now with the reputation of being a really bad lad.

One day, however, things changed dramatically.

'It was really strange, Derek,' David told me. 'I was walking along with me mate, just talking about this and that and planning our next bit of mischief, when I suddenly felt a really hard slap to the side of my head. It really hurt. I looked at my friend and said, "What was that for?" I was just about to fetch him one back when I realized that he couldn't have done it because he was too far away from me. He'd stopped to light a ciggie and I'd carried on walking, so he was a few yards away.

'We carried on towards me other mate's house, but when he asked me in I told him that I was going home. I needed to have a good think. For some reason that slap around the head affected me more than any copper yelling at me or any court of law sending me down.'

Over the next few days David told me that he had stayed in and pondered on his life. He realized that he was not happy at all with his lifestyle and in fact was beginning to feel rather ashamed of himself and the things he had done. He began to look at things from the perspective of those who had suffered because of his actions – the owners of the cars he had stolen, the people whose lives had been affected by his crass and sometimes cruel behaviour. He began to feel deeply ashamed.

'There was nothing I could do to make things better for them, Derek,' he told me, 'but I made a pact with myself that I wouldn't knowingly cause hurt or harm to anybody else.'

David turned over a new leaf. He had lost his opportunity of education by now, for he was 16 years of age, but what he did was find himself a job in a local factory. He started earning a regular wage and mixing with a different group of people socially. He left his old life behind and became a worthwhile member of the community. 'I'm not saying I became a pillar of society, mate,' he said, 'but at least I could look myself in the eye and wasn't dodging out of the way of the coppers!'

David continued to work at the factory. He became a supervisor – a position he still holds – and he has now married and has children of his own. 'And I make sure they keep to the straight and narrow,' he told me with a twinkle in his eye. 'It's funny, y'know, Derek! If I hadn't had had that slap around the ear that day I don't think I'd have stopped what I was doing. I'd just have carried on and ended up being a real no-hoper. Who d'you think it was?'

I smiled. 'That was your guardian angel,' I told him. 'A life of crime wasn't meant for you. You weren't meant to waste your time in prison. You had far more to offer than that. In your old life you wouldn't have met your wife and you wouldn't have brought your children into this life. You were made to change your ways so that you could meet your destiny!'

CHAPTER 4

Spiritual Intervention

There have been many occasions when people have related to me that they have felt that they have been prevented from being involved in an accident or harmed in some way by an unseen force. These are examples of spiritual intervention – those times when it is absolutely evident, without a shadow of doubt, that something or somebody has stepped in and saved us from a dangerous or even fatal situation.

It has to be understood, though, that spiritual intervention can only take place when an injurious event is about to take place that is not on our designated pathway, i.e. is not part of our destiny. If we have chosen to undergo an experience then that event will take place, and nothing and nobody, neither in the physical nor spiritual world, can alter that fact. As explained earlier, we have to meet our destiny in order to achieve soul growth.

There are times, however, when we can be in the wrong place at the wrong time and it is then that our guides, protectors and family members in spirit are allowed to intervene in order to prevent either physical or psychological harm from happening to us.

It may be on the pathway of one person to experience a fatal accident, for example, but not on ours. This is the reason why you read in newspapers of accidents where people 'miraculously escaped'. It is simply the case that whilst one person had chosen to experience that method of passing back to the world of spirit, the other(s) involved had not.

A typical example of spiritual intervention took place in my own and Gwen's life a little while after my mother-in-law, Joanie, passed on to the world of spirit. Gwen and I were preparing to go on a journey which involved driving along quite a large section of the M6. We had been on our journey for no longer than a few minutes and were stationary at a set of traffic lights when the car's engine cut out. No matter what I did, that car was just going nowhere. Ultimately, the garage had to be called out and the car towed back for investigation. An examination of the vehicle could give no particular reason for the engine's refusal to start, but it did uncover a major mechanical fault. If Gwen and I had undertaken that journey it was inevitable that an accident would have occurred that would have resulted in either serious injury or a fatality. As soon as I heard the mechanic's report, I knew that spiritual intervention had taken place and I also felt sure that Joanie had more than a little to do with that intervention!

I do not think that any of us will forget 7 July 2005 – the day when London was almost brought to a standstill by the horrific suicide bombings on the city's transport system. On that day I was travelling to London with Gwen to attend meetings that day and the next. We had elected to fly down from Manchester airport to Heathrow on the 8.30 a.m. flight, so were unaware of what had happened until we actually landed at Heathrow some time after 9 a.m. The airport was in uproar with people trying to get transport into the city. The underground trains had been suspended – due to 'an electrical problem' we were told at the time – and consequently the queues for taxis were enormous. We were more than grateful that a car had been arranged to collect us from the airport. It was only when we climbed into the back of the car that we learned from the driver the true horror of what had taken place during the brief time we had been in the air.

It was a very long slow drive into London along the M4, but as we drew closer to the city on the A4 the traffic became lighter and lighter – a phenomenon we had never experienced before. However, the traffic travelling in the opposite direction was almost gridlocked, such was the desire of people to put as many miles as possible between themselves and the horrors that had so recently taken place. The police were advising people not to travel into London if they could possibly help it, but we had no option. Even though by now all our meetings had been cancelled for that day we still had people to see early the following day and were booked into a hotel for the night.

We eventually arrived at the hotel and with most of the day stretching out in front of us and nothing else to do we decided that after lunch we would take a walk along Oxford Street. However, this was not the Oxford Street we were used to! Most of the shops and restaurants were closed. Because the whole of the transport system had been suspended and taxis were virtually impossible to get, people had left work early to walk home – some of them facing a trek of miles on foot.

Gwen and I wandered aimlessly along, glad to be out of the confines of our hotel. The only people around seemed to be hurrying along with resigned expressions on the faces, no doubt on the way to their homes, and groups of bewildered tourists standing at the barricaded entrances to Oxford Circus and Marble Arch tube stations. Police vehicles rushed by in enormous numbers and there was the incessant sound of sirens screaming.

After a while we turned around and headed back in the direction of our hotel. Turning into a small side street, we noticed that a small coffee shop was still open for business. I ordered coffee for both of us and we sat outside on the almost deserted pavement.

A well-dressed man who looked to be in his thirties was sitting at one of the tables smoking a cigarette with an empty coffee cup in front of him. After a while he picked up his briefcase and began to walk away. After a few paces he hesitated, turned around and approached the table at which Gwen and I were sitting.

'I'm so terribly sorry to bother you, but are you Derek Acorah?' he asked.

I told him that I was.

'I hope you don't mind me speaking to you,' he continued, 'but may I introduce myself and could I ask you a question?'

'Certainly,' I told him.

He pulled out a chair and sat down. I could see that he looked rather upset and decided that I would let him speak without interruption.

The man told me that his name was Craig. He worked in the city and usually travelled via the train and underground system each day. The previous evening he had begun worrying about his journey to work the following day. He had not been able to dismiss these unaccustomed feelings of unease and foreboding, and had even mentioned them to his wife. She had dismissed his worries as being due to pressure of work and the fact that he had an important meeting to attend the following morning.

After a restless night Craig climbed into his car as usual to drive the mile or so to the station. Although his car was not an old one by any means, it had refused to start. Frustrated at the thought of being late for his meeting, Craig ran back into the house and telephoned for a taxi to take him to the station. The taxi duly arrived, but because of unusually heavy traffic the journey took 10 minutes longer than it ought to have done. Craig arrived at the station just in time to see the train he regularly caught disappearing out of the station on its way to London.

'The point is, Derek,' he said, 'had I caught that train I would have been involved in the bombings. I would have been on the very train that was blown up. I might have been in one of the carriages that were so badly affected. I might even have been killed!'

Craig continued by explaining that he had never really considered the reality of the spirit world or the fact that we have people looking after us in another dimension. He told me that although he had watched *Most Haunted* from time to time he had found it merely an entertaining programme and had not dreamed for one moment that the events that took place were real.

'My wife believes everything that happens in the programme, but I've always told her that it's a load of nonsense,' he said, looking more than a little embarrassed. 'Today, however, I've had to seriously consider that there may well be somebody up there looking after me. I cannot explain the feelings I experienced last night and the urge to call into work to say that I wouldn't be coming in today. I'm not the sort of person who would do that, so I overcame my feelings. Then there was the business with the car not starting and, even stranger, the taxi taking so long to get to the station. It's just unknown. I was so angry when I missed that train. Of course when I arrived at the point where I would pick up the tube and found everything was cancelled, the light began to dawn, especially when I heard talk of bombings. Could it be that my guardian angel was trying to get a message to me and I ignored it, so he made sure that I wouldn't be harmed?'

'I think you've answered your own question,' I told Craig. 'It was indeed your guardian angel or, as I call them, your spirit guide impressing you with the fact that all was not well and that you were in danger. It is not on your life's pathway to suffer great physical harm and it is certainly not your time to pass to the world of spirit. Every obstacle possible was put in your way to prevent you from boarding that train this morning.'

'Thank you, Derek,' Craig said as he stood up to take his leave. 'Maybe I'll watch your work in future through newly enlightened eyes,' he added with a smile.

Numerous people have related similar stories to me concerning times when the intervention of somebody not of this world has been evident during a time of potential danger.

Linda wrote to tell me about her experience. She has a daughter, Becky. After Becky was born, Linda developed a strange fear of the staircase leading down from the front door of her apartment to the exterior door. Every time she passed the stairs with her baby in her arms she felt that someone or something was pulling her towards it. It reached a point where if Linda was carrying Becky in the area of the stairs she would walk so that her back was literally rubbing against the opposite wall. If Becky was not with her, nothing would happen and she could quite easily walk by or up and down the stairs without any problem whatsoever.

As Becky grew and began to be more mobile her parents purchased a baby walker. (These baby walkers are now no longer manufactured because they caused so many accidents.) They also positioned a baby gate across the top of the stairs in order to prevent Becky from going anywhere near them.

One day Linda's husband had gone downstairs and unfortunately not locked the baby gate correctly. Linda was in the kitchen. Suddenly she had an overwhelming feeling of fear and dread. She rushed to the stairway in time to see Becky heading downstairs in her walker. What should have happened is that she should have tumbled over and over head over heels many times. Linda was incredulous when she saw her sliding down the stairs instead, still seated securely in her baby walker whilst remaining upright with little more than a gentle bump as she hit each stair.

'It was as though an invisible hand was holding her upright until she reached the bottom of the stairs, where they turned a corner at a 90-degree angle,' she told me.

The baby walker with Becky still in it came to a halt at the bottom of that first set of stairs. During that brief period, Linda managed to reach her daughter and pull her out of the walker before it tumbled down the remaining few steps. Although Becky was screaming with fright, she appeared to be unharmed by her experience.

As a matter of caution Linda and her husband rushed their baby to hospital, where she was X-rayed a number of times. No injuries could be found other than a slight bruise on her forehead.

'Was she just very lucky or was there divine help?' Linda asked me. 'Was it Becky's guardian angel warning me about those stairs when she was a tiny baby, and was she somehow saved from major injury?'

I have to agree with Linda that it is very likely that someone in the world of spirit was looking out for the little girl that day. Somebody intervened to prevent her from being seriously hurt. It is my opinion that it would be a member of Linda's family who had passed to the world of spirit who was impressing Linda with feelings of dread and fear every time she went close to the staircase with her baby in her arms. That person could see what would happen at some point in the future and was determined that Linda would be alert to the possibility of a disaster involving her child and the staircase.

* * *

Catherine is a well-travelled lady who has had numerous experiences where spiritual intervention has prevented her from suffering as a consequence of major riots and bombs. She believes that the number of times this has happened is far too many for it to be purely coincidence.

Once she was travelling to South Africa with her grandparents. A few moments after they left Cape Town serious riots broke out and many people were hurt.

Another time Catherine attempted to book a holiday to Erie in Pennsylvania. She intended to fly on 1 September and return on 11 September, but the travel agent told her that she could only fly via New York City. Again, this trip was to be taken with her grandparents. One had a heart condition and the other was disabled. Catherine demanded that they fly via Pittsburgh and the only flight available was on 10 September. When she and her family arrived back in the UK on 11 September 2001, suicide bombers had attacked America. If she had not been influenced to change the date of their journey, she would have been stranded in New York City with her grandparents.

When in Spain on the Costa del Sol, Catherine intended going to Marbella for the day but then just did not feel right about it. She decided to go to the local market instead and travel to Marbella later in the day. About an hour later, she heard what she thought was a car backfiring. The news came through that a bomb had gone off in the bus station in Marbella, right next to the bus that Catherine would have been on.

Catherine tells me that there have been many, many more instances when she has felt that she is being watched over from the world of spirit. I can do nothing other than agree wholeheartedly that this is definitely the case!

Mandy's mother has a theory that Mandy's friend who passed on to the spirit world in November 1998 saved Mandy's life. Her father, however, is convinced that she is just the luckiest person on Earth.

Mandy's story begins when she was a 16-year-old student at Tooele High School. She was always involved in various events and during the school holidays was required to attend practice for the drill team at 6 a.m. each morning. She lived approximately seven miles from the high school and her journey involved passing the Tooele Army Depot main entrance.

As well as being part of the drill team, Mandy was also performing in a musical called *The Benson Gristmill Pageant*. On the final night of the pageant, she stayed out until around 4 a.m. at a cast party. Then she went home, but had to be up again at 5.45 a.m. to attend her drill practice.

Normally when Mandy would drive to drill practice there was a lot of traffic, because the army depot shift began around 6 a.m., but on this particular morning there were no other cars on the road. That was just as well, because after about three or four miles Mandy fell asleep. She was woken up by the sound of rocks hitting the windows of the car as they were thrown up by the tyres. She realized that she was about to hit a reflector pole head on, so swerved, but unfortunately the pole hit the passenger side of the car. This caused it to spin out of control.

As Mandy battled to gain control of the vehicle once more, she continued sideways along a fence and turned the car again just before she hit a telephone cable pole. By this time the brakes had failed. Mandy slid past another sign and all the way across the road where there was a steep drop. With no brakes, it was impossible for her to stop the car. Just before it reached the drop, however, the front tyres blew and the vehicle came to a halt.

Mandy says that the car was 'totalled'. All four wheel rims were bent, the frame was damaged, there was no front passenger door, no mirrors, no windows on the passenger side and no door handles. The engine had been shoved up the dashboard right to the point of entering the front seat.

Mandy had not even been wearing a seatbelt, but she walked away from the car with only a small cut and a strained ligament in her left foot. When the police arrived they were amazed that she had come out of the accident alive, particularly because she was so close to the busy army depot.

Mandy says that she is not sure what happened that day, but having three police officers point out about half a dozen reasons why you should be dead or seriously injured really has the effect of waking you up.

I have to agree with Mandy's mother – on that day Mandy was certainly being looked after by spirit. It may well have been her friend, but could also have been a member of her family who was looking down upon her.

I hope that in future Mandy will remember that driving when you are as tired as she was really is a very dangerous thing to do and gives all those people in the spirit world who care for us an awful lot of extra work.

Christine is convinced that an angel saved her daughter's life whilst she was out on a shopping trip.

At the time Christine was standing next to the car with her daughter whilst her husband returned to the shop to pick a few things up. As he came out of the shop his daughter saw him and set off running to meet him in between the parked cars. Christine panicked, as she could see a car moving at some speed through the rows of cars, looking for somewhere to park. Before she had a chance to call out to her daughter to stop, 'it was like she had run into a wall and she was thrown back, inches away from the car she was about to collide with. She landed on her bottom. I just knew that something had stopped her suddenly and thankfully saved my child.'

Christine says that although there was no visual evidence of an angel being present, in her heart she knows that something extraordinary happened on that day.

Trent was on a camping trip with his family and friends. They were staying in a log cabin close to a rocky ridge.

When the family had settled into their cabin, Trent and his father went exploring. Trent decided that he would go down a slope very carefully and slowly, but unfortunately at one point leaned too far forward and was propelled at full speed almost to the brink of a precipice. Suddenly he felt an 'amazing swooping sensation' which knocked him back. It felt as though an 'amazing strength' had come from someone who was looking down on him and protecting him.

Paul wrote to tell me of an incident that happened when he was driving along in his car. The radio began to crackle badly and he pulled over to tune it in, thus delaying his journey by a few short moments.

With the radio working properly once more, he set off once more. As he approached a set of traffic lights, he was horrified to see a vehicle drive through the red lights straight across his pathway. Had he not stopped momentarily to tune in his radio he would have been in the direct pathway of this vehicle and would have been severely injured or even killed.

Another incident involving driving was reported by Holly. She was driving her car along a motorway in a convoy of traffic which included a large articulated lorry, when for no apparent reason she felt compelled to turn off at the next exit. Even as she was doing so she just could not understand why she was feeling this compulsion. Feeling rather annoyed with herself because she now had to find her way back to the motorway using a network of A roads and had added time to her journey, she drove on for about three miles before finding signs back to the motorway.

As she approached the sliproad, however, she was caught in a tailback of traffic and could see blue lights flashing ahead. As the queue of traffic progressed slowly onto the motorway she could see that there had been an accident involving the very same articulated lorry and group of vehicles in which she had earlier been travelling. Had she not pulled off the motorway, she too would have been involved in the accident.

Somebody was obviously looking after Holly, because not too long after the above incident, she was distraught to realize that she had lost a considerable sum of money whilst working on a film shoot in a large muddy field. The money was to pay for her food for the next week and without it she would not be able to eat. She was absolutely desperate.

After work, as she was walking along the street to her flat, she saw a lottery ticket on the floor and felt compelled to pick it up. She went into her home and turned on the television just in time to see that four of the numbers on the ticket she had found had been drawn that night in the National Lottery. She hurried around to her local supermarket and proffered the lottery ticket. In return she received a sum of money identical to the amount she had lost earlier in the day.

Kay recalls the time some years ago when she received a telephone call from her mother, Sue, who was very distressed because she had had a dream. In the dream she had seen her own mother, who had passed on to the spirit world some time before, but she would not let her draw close to her. She remained behind what Sue described as a 'veil of sorts' and kept telling her that the time was not right.

Later that day Sue was involved in a horrific motor accident. She was so badly injured that she was not expected to live. She was in a coma and was placed on life support. Her family was told that it might be kinder to switch off the life-support machine.

As Kay sat with her mother, holding her hand and telling her how much she was loved and wanted, a tear rolled down Sue's cheek. Against all the odds, Kay and the rest of the family decided that they would ignore the doctors' advice and keep on fighting for Sue's life.

Weeks passed and slowly Sue began to make a recovery. A year later she was back at home. She recalls very little of what happened on that dreadful day, but does remember that her mother was in constant attendance whilst she was in hospital, telling her that, just as in her dream, the time was not right for her to join her family in the spirit world.

CHAPTER 5

The Words of an Angel

Because mediums are in direct communication with the world of spirit people generally think that we have all the answers and do not experience any of the ups and downs in life. This is just not so. We cannot live our lives isolated from the trials and tribulations of life here on the Earth plane. We get hurt, both physically and emotionally, just as much as other people. We feel let down, we feel emotional pain, we fall in and out of love and we also experience the anguish and grief of losing a loved one to the spirit world. We are of course fortunate in that we know that at some point in the future those loved ones will communicate with us and show themselves to us clairvoyantly, but it is just not the same as throwing your arms around a person here on Earth.

It was at such a low time in my life that I was walking along the sands at Southport. It was late autumn and the town was empty of holiday-makers. Anybody who knows Southport will be aware that the beach is enormous and when the tide is out you are hard pressed to see the waters of the Mersey estuary and the Irish Sea in the distance.

I was feeling very depressed. Life was not being kind to me. Nothing was going right. I had deep financial problems and my emotional life was in a catastrophic state. I felt that I had nothing left to live for. Ending it all and taking myself over to the spirit world seemed a very appealing option.

As I walked towards the murky waters I thought how easy it would be to just keep on walking and to disappear completely from this earthly plane. 'What do I have left to live for?' I asked myself.

It was at this point that I became aware of a young lady walking along beside me about 10 feet distant from me. As I turned my head to look at her, I recognized her. It was my sister Angela.

Angela had but a brief visit to the Earth plane. She had passed to the spirit world as a very young baby and I only had a vague recollection of her coming into our family. My last memory of her was lying in a tiny coffin in my grandmother's front parlour. Throughout my life, however, whenever the going has got tough for me Angela has shown herself and encouraged me to carry on in spite of the difficulties I have been facing at the time. Although only a tiny baby when she passed back to the spirit world, just like me she had grown and matured and was now a lovely young woman who was the image of our own mother when she was in her middle twenties.

Angela smiled reassuringly at me. I could feel the depth of her love and care washing over me.

'The time's not right, Degs,' she said. 'There's somebody out there for you. You'll find love again – somebody who will care for you properly and who'll value you. You don't have much longer to wait. When you meet this person, you'll find every aspect of your life will improve – it'll take on an even keel and everything will balance.'

I ceased my heavy trudging through the wet sand towards the water's edge and looked up towards the dark clouded sky. As I did so, a small chink appeared in the clouds and a beam of watery winter sun shone down upon the waters. I felt a lightening within myself.

I turned to look once more towards Angela. She smiled reassuringly, raised her hand in salute and slowly faded from my sight.

My sister Angela! So well named – an angel indeed! And she was right! Although things did not happen overnight, gradually opportunities presented themselves in my life and I was able to sort out the more pressing problems. I weathered my emotional storm and although it would be more than a year before I found true love once again, I was able to start enjoying myself in the company of friends. I also had my work for spirit – the most important thing in my life. I realized that I needed the time without being tied to an emotional relationship in order to dedicate myself my spiritual work.

The night after my walk on the sands I attended my regular physical circle. Physical circles are meetings of a number of mediums, usually between six and eight, who sit with the sole purpose of assisting one of their numbers to attain physical mediumship. Physical mediumship is the point where a medium goes beyond the gifts of clairaudience, clairvoyance and clairsentience and develops the ability to produce ectoplasm in substantial enough quantities to enable a spirit to be viewed by those who do not have the ability to see clairvoyantly.

The physical circle I was attending was held in the home of my good friend Ray Pugh. Ray was a medium of some repute. As we sat preparing ourselves, he said to me, 'Angela's just called in to say hello. She's glad that you listened to her yesterday. She loves her brother, but she isn't ready to welcome you to the world of spirit just yet.'

I hung my head in shame. I felt desperately embarrassed that Ray knew of my plans the previous day. What would he think of me? Here was I, somebody who was giving spiritual advice to people as they faced the rigours of their earthly life, succumbing to the desire to give up the fight. There were people out there who were far worse off than me, people facing what seemed to be insurmountable problems, looking to me for spiritual advice and I had been contemplating not only letting them down but also the spirit world.

I looked up. Ray was smiling kindly at me. 'I understand, Derek,' he told me. 'Mediums aren't superhuman. We all have our low points, but remember, spirit loves you. You have some special work to do for them. Your sister Angela and your guides and helpers are giving you strength. You'll go on from here and one day you will look back to this day and realize that what you have gone through is a learning process, the better for you to appreciate what spirit has in store. You will do great works and in some way will be a pioneer. Continue on! It is meant!'

I sometimes reflect back to those dark days and think about the wonderful experiences I would have missed out on if I had just walked into the sea. I would not have met the people who have crossed my path and enriched my life in the way that they have. I would have cheated myself out of a wonderful and rewarding marriage. And most importantly of all, at some point in my spiritual existence I would have had to come back and do it all again!

It is not unusual for a person in the spirit world to whisper words of comfort or love to a loved one still living in this physical life, especially at times of stress and hardship. Samantha had such an experience during a journey to the hospital where her father was lying gravely ill.

Samantha knew that recovery for her father was unlikely and was grief-stricken at the thought of losing him. As she and her husband were driving along she heard a voice telling her, 'We will take him.' She knew instantly that the angels were coming for her father that day and started to cry, but when her husband asked her what was wrong, she felt that she could not tell him that she had heard a voice telling her that her father would be leaving his physical life that day.

That evening Samantha's father passed on to the spirit world, but just knowing that the angels were taking care of him was such a comfort to Samantha. She says that she will never forget the message and feels privileged that she received the proof that many people do not.

Since her father passed on to the spirit world, Samantha tells me that she has seen him in spirit and knows that he is happy and cared for in the heavenly state.

Ruth was suffering from depression and was in the depths of despair. She had reached a point where she felt that she could no longer go on. Help came when she was sitting alone in her grandmother's home. She describes feeling as though she was suddenly wrapped up in a warm blanket of love. Then she heard a man's voice calling her name. She says that it was such a kind voice and it kept telling her over and over again that everything was going to be alright.

Another person who was brought back from the brink was Eddie. He had been involved in an unsuccessful marriage and seriously thought that his only way out was to take his own life.

As he walked crying towards his bedroom in the now-empty house he suddenly noticed a beautiful smell of flowers. He suddenly felt so calm and relaxed, he stopped crying. He felt as though someone was holding him and wrapping him up in an atmosphere of love. He heard a quiet voice calling his name and speaking to him. Realization of how selfish it would be to take his own life suddenly dawned. He had three children who would be bereft if he was no longer around. His parents and the rest of his family loved him. How could he cause such hurt to them?

So often people in the spirit world whisper words of comfort to us at just the right moment.

CHAPTER 6

Do Angels Follow You Wherever You Go?

It is true to say that there is always somebody from the spirit world looking over us. They may not be always by our side, but you can be assured that the moment anything of potential hurt or harm, whether physical or emotional, enters our lives they are right there beside us.

As I have explained previously, some things are meant to be. We have chosen a particular direction or experience in order to further our soul growth, and in those instances our guardians cannot interfere. What they can do, however, is give us courage in our chosen times of hardship and be close to us and help with an easy transition back to the world of spirit if that is our choice. They can also support us through emotional hurt. Even though we may be unaware of it at the time, they are always there.

Sometimes we may wonder whether we are taking the correct steps on our pathway. But if we listen to our own inner voice, it will keep telling us to take the steps we have been thinking of, to make that move we have been craving. It is all meant to be.

I had not seen Tony for over a year, but he visited me one day during the time when I had an office in Liverpool city centre. He asked me whether I had time to listen to a very strange story.

Tony explained to me that he had finally made up his mind and moved to Canada. He had been thinking about it for years but had done nothing about it, even though the desire to do so kept nagging at him. Close members of his family had taken the decision to move some nine years earlier, but at that time he had wanted to remain in England because he had a girlfriend in this country and did not want to leave her behind.

Tony explained that for the six months or so prior to emigrating he had been having some very strange dreams. In one dream he had seen his mother and father and the rest of his family who were now in Canada in what looked like a frozen park. They seemed to be very happy, laughing and joking, as they all tried to ice skate. Tony explained that sometimes the setting of his dream was at night-time, as he could see scattered lights around the icy area, whilst on other occasions it was daytime. In each and every dream, however, he would always hear his dad saying out loud, 'I really wish our Tony was here with us!'

Tony telephoned his mother to tell her about his dream. She told him that she and his father made a practice of going to an ice rink every Sunday morning and sometimes on a Thursday evening and that it was an open-air ice rink in a public park. She also told him that his father often commented that he wished Tony could be with them because he knew that his son would enjoy it so much.

A second dream that Tony told me about was quite scary. It was set in a room. He did not know where that room was, but his mother, father and family were sitting around a table eating. There was music playing in the background and everybody was having a happy time until he heard his mother ask his father what was wrong. Then Tony saw his father lying on the floor with the rest of the family milling around him in obvious distress. The dream would then cut to another scene where his family was enjoying a barbecue by a huge lake. Tony tried to talk to them, but they could not hear him and certainly gave no indication that they could see him. Once more the dream would suddenly end with his father lying on the floor.

After both dreams Tony would always wake up in a lather of sweat and with a feeling of panic. 'As you know, Derek, I'm an ambulance driver, so I don't panic easily, but this!' Because the content of the second dream was so disturbing he decided that he would not share it with his mother for fear of worrying her.

Tony told me that it was because of these vivid dreams that he had finally made up his mind to move to Canada. He had been unsure whether they were a portent of something to come and wanted to be near to his family if that were the case. He had discussed the matter with his fiancée Lisa. Arrangements had already been put in place for their wedding in England, but they made the joint decision to cancel those plans and marry in Canada.

All the arrangements were made and finally Tony and Lisa arrived in Canada, to be met by his mother and father. The first thing that Tony did on seeing his father was to ask whether he was feeling alright. 'Never felt better, son!' his dad exclaimed.

Three months passed. Tony found temporary work as a landscape gardener until a position more suited to his training became available and Lisa started working as a beauty therapist. They were both living their life in

their new country and were due to be married on 22
August, which coincidentally was the same date arranged
for their original wedding in England.

The day finally arrived. The weather was beautiful,
the ceremony went well and afterwards people enjoyed
themselves eating and drinking. Many wandered out onto
the lawn outside the country club where the reception was
being held.

Suddenly Tony heard his mother's voice screaming out,
'Oh no! No! George!' He rushed over to see his father
lying on the ground clutching his chest. He was having a
heart attack! Because of his training Tony was immediately aware of the problem and followed the correct procedures to keep his father as stable as possible until the
ambulance arrived.

George was taken to the hospital with Tony and his
mother in the ambulance beside him. Happily, the medical
team was able to stabilize George, but they told Tony
that without his presence and knowledge of the correct
procedures, the outcome would probably not have been
so good.

'It's strange, isn't it, Derek?' Tony said. 'I've always had
this nagging feeling that I should go and live in Canada,
but it was those dreams which really gave me the push.
I wouldn't have gone if it hadn't have been for them. I'd

probably have put it off and put it off until in the end I would have been too old.'

I raised my eyebrows and smiled. I well knew the workings of spirit.

The story had not ended, though. A few weeks after Tony's wedding he was visiting his parents' house. While he was there his mother was speaking on the telephone to a relative who lived in England in the same area where Tony had been living. Afterwards she came into the living room looking white faced. 'You'll never guess what!' she exclaimed. 'The hall where you'd booked your wedding reception in England has blown up. There was a gas leak or something and it has been completely destroyed by the explosion. And d'you know when it happened?'

Tony shook his head.

'At 3.30 p.m. on 22 August!' she replied. 'Exactly the time that we would have been sitting down to your wedding breakfast!'

'So what d'you think of that?' Tony asked me. 'Me moving to Canada because of dreams I'd been having – and those dreams coming true! If I hadn't have been there my father would probably not be with us now, and if we'd been married in England, we'd all have been blown up! Somebody's definitely looking after us!'

I agreed with Tony. Somebody had definitely been looking after him and his family and they had followed them to Canada to do so. That family's guardian angels are certainly very well travelled!

Chapter 7

Do Angels Meet Us When We Die?

So, spirit guides are with us throughout our earthly lives, but what happens when the time to leave this mortal life arrives? What exactly do we experience at that moment when we leave our world to travel on to the next? Do angels meet us when we die?

Although it may sound terribly appealing, I am afraid that there are no banks of winged angels heralding our arrival into the spirit world with celestial tunes played on long golden bugles. There is no heavily bearded Saint Peter, guardian of the pearly gates, waiting with a large book in hand to hold us accountable for all our earthly deeds.

At the moment of physical death the spirit self detaches itself from the earthly body. Mediums who have been present at such a time have described seeing the spirit person rise from the physical body. As the spirit form gently rises, a silver cord linking them to their body becomes taut and then breaks, leaving the spirit free to float upwards and on to the realms beyond from whence it came.

At that very moment in time the person's spirit guide is standing very close by in a bright beautiful light. In the background are the person's relatives and friends. No fear or dubiousness is felt by the person rejoining them, only an overwhelming sensation of love and a desire to step forward into that miraculous light.

As we step forward, our spirit guide gently explains to us that our lifetime on the earthly plane is spent and it is time to rejoin our spirit family. A wonderful time of reunion is enjoyed with all those we have loved on the Earth plane and who have passed on to the spirit world before us and then we are taken to a place where we can rest and recuperate from the rigours of our life here on Earth. We go into a prolonged period of what I call the 'sleep state'. The length of time we spend recuperating depends entirely on our experiences just prior to and at the moment of our physical death. If we have suffered a long and protracted illness, then the time we spend in the sleep state will be longer than if we, say, pass on to the spirit world as the result of a sudden heart attack which has brought us over quickly.

Once we awaken from the sleep state we are taken to exactly where we want to be. If it is our desire to dwell in a rose-covered cottage, then that is where we will be. If we wish to experience the wild ocean as our daily companion, then this wish will be granted. In other words, we live in exactly the conditions our spirit selves consider to be perfection. We can spend our time with people we have loved in our earthly life and can be reunited with our beloved pets, those animals who meant so much to us when they shared their time on Earth with us. We can visit the people we left behind on the Earth plane who are still living their earthly lives and as we progress, we may, if we wish, allow those people to become aware that we are still around them. We can help them in ways that we could not before by influencing their thoughts when they are about to make decisions which may not have the best outcome for them. We can put things right in a way that we were not able to do before, but what we cannot do is interfere with their own free will, nor can we alter their earthly pathway and take away from them the experiences they chose to undergo before they incarnated into physical life. We can be there to greet them when the time comes for them to join us, but we cannot alter the fact that that meeting may come in their childhood, adolescence or early adulthood. It is not meant for everybody to live to a grand old age and die peacefully in their sleep.

There are of course exceptions to every rule and although what I have described above is generally the system of things when a person leaves their physical life, there are always those who choose not to step into the light offered to them upon the moment they leave their physical bodies.

Some people, once in spirit form, choose to remain close to the Earth plane for a number of days or even weeks before they finally decide to finally pass on to the spirit world. These people may wish to spend a little longer close to the family they have left behind. They feel the grief of the family they have left and that grief and longing make it more difficult for them to leave the earthly atmosphere. It is at such times that I have had people say to me that the 'ghost' of a deceased person has been seen at their own funeral, or that Great-aunt Annie was seen sitting in her favourite chair only the day after she passed to spirit!

Then there are the people who, because of what they have done here on Earth, are afraid to pass on to the next world for fear of what will happen to them. These people may have committed a heinous crime or any number of horrible acts against humankind. So they stay put or remain 'grounded' here and generally maintain the same type of personality they had whilst living here in the physical world.

Of course, once they do move on into the spirit world, their lot is not the same as that of a person who has lived a relatively blameless life and has not gone out of their way to do anyone harm. Like attracts like and the people who have committed horrible wrongs will spend their time in the lower realms of the spirit world with spirit people of similar nature. From time to time, however, they will be given the opportunity to atone for their actions and therefore the opportunity to progress into the true light.

I conducted a sitting some time ago for a mother whose daughter had been viciously murdered. I am using fictitious names to protect the identity of the people involved. I was fortunate in that I was able to bring the young girl Lydia through during that sitting. I was able to assure her mother Nicole that she was safe and well in the world of spirit and being looked after by her grandmother, who had passed away only months before the terrible event took place. She was happy to be reunited through my mediumship with the mother she had left behind in the physical world.

Nicole was overjoyed at the communication. She had visited me only weeks after the tragic event had taken place and I had had to explain to her then that the likelihood of Lydia coming through was slim because it was so soon after her passing. It was more than likely that she would still be recuperating.

'Would it be possible for you to ask Lydia who met her at heaven's gate?' Nicole asked me. 'I often worry about that. I couldn't stand the thought of her being met by strangers and being afraid.'

I closed my eyes in concentration and asked Sam whether it would be possible to bring Lydia forward once more.

After a few moments I heard a tinkling laugh. 'I know what Mum's been asking you,' said Lydia's voice. 'Tell her that Grandma was there to meet me. Uncle Tim came too, as well as Cassie and Bonnie! There were quite a few people I didn't recognize, but they were all very nice to me.'

I related the information to Nicole, who smiled when I mentioned Cassie and Bonnie. 'They were two little Jack Russell dogs we'd had since before Lydia was born. She loved them to bits and was heartbroken when they died. Lydia's Uncle Tim was my brother, who we lost four years ago. He was quite a bit older than me, but not old enough to go the way he did with a heart attack! I'm so happy she wasn't frightened and that Mam was there for her.'

Nicole was just about to leave my office when she suddenly sat down again with a worried expression on her face. 'One more thing, Derek! That bastard who did for her – he committed suicide not long after, you know. He won't be in heaven with my Lydia, will he? There's no chance he'd bump into her and frighten her again, is there? Surely after what he's done he wouldn't be in the same place as my innocent girl who never did any harm to anybody?'

I was able to explain to Nicole that the person who had been responsible for murdering Lydia would certainly not be dwelling in the same realms as her daughter. He would have gone to a lower realm and would be residing there with like-minded people until the time came when he had truly repented of his deeds. To do this he would have to reincarnate into the physical world once more and choose one of two pathways – either he would have to dedicate a lifetime to helping others with no particular reward or he would have to suffer a physical life of hardship in whatever way it was considered just and fit by the hierarchy of the spirit world. It would take a very long time for that person to repay the karmic debt he had incurred by viciously taking away Lydia's physical life.

CHAPTER 8

Near-Death Experience

A common description given by people who have approached death is of travelling rapidly down a dark tunnel at the end of which shines a brilliant white light. They may note that as they travel down the tunnel, or even at the end of the tunnel, they see members of their family who have previously passed on to the spirit world. Their descriptions of these family members may vary from their last memory of that person to how they looked whilst in the prime of life.

A young lady who had experienced such a near-death experience told me that she felt as though she had 'passed out'. During the time that she was unconscious she felt as though she was walking down a corridor. She could see people she knew who had passed on to the spirit world, such as her grandmother and her great-grandmother. She tried to talk to them, but they did not answer. She remembers crying out to her grandmother, telling her that she had to join her, but her grandmother saying, 'You cannot! You can't come with me.'

Teresa was the victim of a terrible knife attack. Whilst lying in the back of the ambulance as the paramedics attended to her, she was on the verge of passing to spirit. She had given up and did not want to live any longer. Whilst in the ambulance the voices of the crew faded and became very distant and Teresa found herself surrounded by a bright light. At the same moment she heard a strong voice telling her that everything would be alright – and it was. She opened her eyes and told the ambulance crew that she was alright.

During such an experience some people will not record having been spoken to whilst others will remember being told 'No! It's not your time. You have to go back.' And this is the crux of the matter. Near-death experiences are just that – near death! The time is not right for full transition to the world of spirit. What a person is undergoing is one of *life's* experiences and they have to carry on living in the physical world until it is their correct time for passing.

Some people may undergo a number of serious accidents or dangerous incidents and will survive to carry on with their physical lives. The results of those incidents may impair their physical ability to live their lives as before, but that is what they have chosen to undergo on their life's pathway in order to achieve soul growth in the next life. Other people may experience just one accident and will pass to spirit as a result. It is all down to our own personal choice, but at the end of the day we pass on to the spirit world when the time is right and no sooner.

In some instances people have described a situation where they have left their physical body and been floating around somewhere near the ceiling or in another part of the room, looking down at their physical form lying on a bed. They may have suffered some form of trauma and the situation may well be a hospital room. Or they may have merely retired for the night and suddenly become aware that they are no longer curled up asleep but watching their body lying on the bed.

This is not a near-death experience but an 'out-of-body experience' brought about by the detachment of the spirit self from the physical self. There are those who have become able to control this out-of-body state and practise it as a form of meditation.

Drew speaks about an experience he had when he was a boy of six and was lying on the sofa at home one sunny afternoon. He was feeling quite tired, but this was not abnormal for him as he had been quite poorly with asthma. In fact he had been in and out of hospital quite frequently because of the condition.

Drew tells me that as he lay on the sofa he suddenly had the impression that he was on top of the moors near to where he lived. He remembers feeling the sun on his face and the wind in his hair. He realized that he was floating in a position that he describes as 'feet pointing downwards and my arms outstretched, about four feet above the ground'.

As Drew looked to his left he could see a multi-coloured mass coming towards him from the other side of a hill. This mass was similar to a rainbow but with all the colours interchanging. It was about five feet high and roughly the same shape as a human. The colours were moving erratically and seemed hazy. The mass stopped about 30 yards away from Drew. Although it had no face, Drew knew that it was smiling at him. He describes feeling a love that was total and unconditional. No words were spoken, but Drew had the feeling that the message 'I'm watching over you, don't worry' was being conveyed to him.

The next thing Drew knew was that he was back on the sofa once more as though nothing had happened. Soon after this incident, the asthmatic condition from which he suffered went away and did not return.

Drew concludes by saying, 'The funny thing about this experience is that I get more comfort from it now than when it actually happened. I was too young to understand the experience and it is only these past years that I have drawn strength from it. Whatever it was, it has had a lovely impact on my life.'

Lucy wrote to tell me about her experience whilst in hospital having just given birth to a stillborn child. She was in both mental and physical pain and effectively shut herself off from the outside world. She says that she had a feeling of floating above everyone watching them trying to console her.

Eventually she reached a point where she began to be able to cry. As she lay there grief-stricken in her hospital bed one night a beautiful smell seemed to fill the air around her. It made her feel happy and loved. A woman pulled the hospital curtain back and Lucy assumed that she was one of the nurses. When she looked through the darkness, though, she saw that the woman was not wearing a uniform but just a simple long-sleeved tunic.

The woman took Lucy's hand and told her, 'You're going to be fine.' Her aura was such that it gave her a sense of love, peace and harmony. She then walked away, but to Lucy's surprise, there was no sound of footsteps on the hard hospital floor.

Happily, a year later, Lucy gave birth to a baby boy. Although she will never forget the circumstances surrounding the birth of her first child, her little boy has brought her much joy and happiness.

'Astral travel' is where the spirit self leaves the physical body to travel through the astral planes. This is achieved through deep meditation and should not be attempted by everyone.

Astral travel allows a person to travel in spirit form to just about any place they wish to go. The experience is mind-boggling and can only be described as flying just as a bird flies, though without the obvious physical effort. It allows a person to drift across countries not visited before, visit sites unseen by the physical eye and to visit the lower, gruesome astral planes of the spirit world. People would obviously not do this through choice, though it can sometimes occur involuntarily during sleep. Then a person will wake up having had a 'nightmare' where they felt that they were in a place where horrendous creatures dwelt and inhuman things were taking place.

'Remote viewing' is travelling astrally to a place with the sole purpose of viewing that place, be it an office, a home, etc. People may claim to practise it, but great care should be exercised when listening to such claims. I have heard of many where the 'remote viewing' is basically a combination of guesswork and cold reading, and I have also had to deal with so many cases where people have been frightened out of their wits by the thought that another person can just come along and spy on them at will.

I have to add here that most of these bogus claims of remote viewing are made on the internet. I would therefore advise everybody to shun any claims that people can glide through cyberspace and land neatly on the sofa next to you.

CHAPTER 9

Soul Growth

I have mentioned the term 'soul growth' many times during the previous chapters. I would like now to explain exactly what I mean by that term.

Before we incarnate into our earthly life, before we are even physically conceived, when our spirits are still resident in the world beyond, we are given choices. Those choices concern our lives on the Earth plane – what we want to achieve, the experiences we wish to undergo and what we want to make of ourselves. The ultimate aim for any spirit is to ascend to the higher spiritual realms. To achieve this we have to ensure that we have had as many experiences as we possibly can – good or bad – in our earthly incarnations. The harsher the experience, the higher our true self climbs on the spiritual ladder. When we have experienced everything, both good and bad, then we remain in the world of spirit, dwelling in the higher realms forever.

I am often asked why innocent babies and young people have to go through horrendous events in their short lifetimes here on Earth, why some young lives are cut short by either accidents or acts of malice or cruelty by another person, why some children succumb to illnesses which take them back to the spirit world at an early age, why hundreds of thousands of young lives are cut short due to famine, disease or natural disaster. The answer is simple: those young souls chose to undergo those experiences before they incarnated here on Earth. And why? To take their spirit selves further up the spiritual ladder and closer to the ultimate heavenly state.

In subsequent incarnations they may choose an easier lifetime here on Earth. They may choose to be born into a loving family, wanting for nothing and with a relatively trouble-free and long lifespan. After such a life they will still become closer to the Godhead when their time comes to pass back to the spirit world, but they will only have climbed one rung as opposed to the many rungs they climbed in their harsher existence.

During my professional career as a spirit medium I have on more than one occasion been approached by the parent or parents of a child who has passed over to the world of spirit as a result of having their physical life taken away from them by another person. The parents left behind find it beyond their comprehension that their son or daughter may have chosen to experience passing back to the spirit world in such a gruesome manner. It is, however, true that the spirit of their child chose to experience that particular method of passing. They chose it for their soul growth, just as the spirit selves of the parents chose to experience the loss of a child in a violent way. In both cases, because of the extreme grief and trauma involved, many rungs of the spiritual ladder are climbed.

Similarly, people may view suicide as an 'opting out' of life's more difficult times. This is not so. The spirit person, before being born, chose to take themselves back to the spirit world in what some people would term an 'untimely death'.

To take another example, a husband and father may return to the spirit world whilst still relatively young. In this case, not only did his spirit choose to experience an early passing but the spirit of his wife and children chose to undergo bereavement before they, too, incarnated on this Earth plane.

Each of us is intrinsically linked and we help those with whom we come into contact in order to achieve our life's destiny. We may not know it, but that is exactly what we are doing. Everything is meant, whether we like it or not. And we are the people who chose the course of our lifetime here on Earth, nobody else.

I am sure that everybody has at some time heard the statement 'Oh, they're an old soul' or 'They've been here before!' being made about a small child or a baby. And it is true. We have all been here before in different times and in different ages. Some have had more incarnations than others – these are the 'old souls'. Some spirits may wait many hundreds of our earthly years before returning to the physical world. It is always a matter of choice – our choice! We come when we please and we make our own decision as to how long we live our lives in the physical world and what we will experience whilst we are here.

CHAPTER 10

The Wrong Pathway

Though we have chosen our life's pathway before incarnation, sometimes we are determined not to follow it! We think that we know what is best for us and studiously ignore our own inner voice. We are determined that we will do what we want to do.

We may be allowed by our guides and helpers to carry on for a while on the wrong pathway, but sooner or later we will be forced to step into the life that is meant for us. If we keep ignoring the signals along the way, then our situation will become harder and harder for us. We will eventually reach a point where we will have to sit up and take notice and get on with the life that is intended for us.

* * *

I had completed one of my theatre shows and was having a quick cup of tea in my dressing room before returning to the front of house to do signings. Whilst I was in the dressing room the manager of the theatre came along and handed me a letter. Upon reading it I became very concerned and anxious. Fortunately the man who had written the letter had given his name, Simon, and his telephone number. I vowed that the following day I would contact him.

Simon had written to tell me that for years he had followed a pathway of spiritual growth and had developed his mediumistic gifts in order to help people with his insights. About two years earlier his younger sister, who was also a budding medium, had passed to the spirit world as a result of a tragic accident. Ever since her passing everything had seemed to go awry. Simon said that it had reached the stage where every time he went to bed and fell asleep he would go into a sequence of dreams. Every one was the same. He would see his sister walking towards him, telling him that it was unfair that he was still in his physical life doing what she wanted to do more than anything else and that it had been her life's ambition to become a fully-fledged medium. The dream would then take on a more sinister tone in that his sister's face would change into something ugly and grotesque. Simon would see a strange creature spitting and snarling at him. At this point he always woke up in a cold sweat.

I telephoned Simon and made arrangements to visit him at his home in the Lancashire area.

When I arrived at the house, before I had even stepped inside, I was aware of an energy which was not at all happy with the fact that I was there. I had the overwhelming impression that I was definitely not a welcome visitor. I could also not pick up any of the usual emanations from Simon that I would expect when in the company of another medium working for the greater good, although I knew that there was definite psychic ability there.

Simon showed me through to his sitting room and asked me to take a seat. As I went to sit down on the sofa, one of the cushions shifted dramatically. Simon went out to the kitchen area to make a cup of tea and whilst he did so I sent out thoughts into the ether enquiring who it was in the spirit world who so desperately did not want me in this home.

I was answered almost immediately by the voice of a lady who introduced herself as Gladys. She said that she and a lady in spirit named Claire were not happy with what was going on and warned me that all was not as it would seem. I received a mental image of Gladys, who seemed to be older and calmer, and Claire, who was very much younger, only around her middle twenties in age, and was much more agitated and upset. I asked Gladys why they were so worried and why they were here, but it was Claire who replied, telling me that she was Simon's sister and that Gladys was their grandmother.

At that point Simon returned to the room with two cups of tea. As we sat and talked I said to him, 'You never did tell me your sister's name, Simon.'

'But I thought you'd know that, Derek,' he said with a smile.

'Oh dear! Here we go!' I thought to myself. I did not think that anybody who was so far forward in his spiritual awareness as Simon claimed to be would be likely to say anything quite so inane as that to another medium. I began to view him in an even more guarded manner and did not mention to him what had happened whilst he was out of the room making the tea.

Simon then smiled and said, 'My sister's name was Claire.'

I asked him what his relationship had been like with his sister before she passed from her physical life. He hesitated, then said that it had been good – that he had loved her and she had loved him. However, I could feel a sense of agitation emanating from him and he became a little twitchy as we talked about his earlier life before he had decided to take his first steps onto a spiritual pathway.

After we had been speaking for a few minutes, Simon said to me, 'Why are we talking about all this? I thought you had come along to help me sort this out!'

Then I told him what I had experienced whilst he had been out of the room.

'I knew that I hadn't been dreaming,' he said. 'I knew that Claire had been visiting me in my sleep.'

I agreed with him that this was so, but by now I was beginning to feel out of sorts for some reason. I felt drained of energy, though there was no reason for me to feel that way.

The conversation continued for another five or ten minutes, but I began to feel so ill that I thought it would be better if I terminated the visit and returned another day. When I suggested this Simon seemed almost relieved. I got the distinct impression that I was touching on something that was making him feel very nervous indeed. I gave him my telephone number and returned to my own home, where I immediately began to feel very much better. Within the hour I was back to normal. I had not made a definite arrangement for a return visit to Simon, but knew that it would not be very long before I heard from him once more.

The following day the telephone rang at my home. It was a very distressed Simon. He was virtually shouting down the line, 'Ever since you came to my house all hell has broken loose!'

He proceeded to tell me that in the evening after my visit during the afternoon, at around 11.45 p.m., he had been watching television when he had heard a large bang coming from the kitchen. He had run into the area and seen the outline of two spirit women standing motionless in the centre of the room. He had backed out into the sitting room, but the two spirit forms had followed him and positioned themselves in front of the fireplace. The lights in the room had flickered, then gone off and come back on again.

Simon told me that he had asked the spirit people who they were because by this time he was feeling quite unnerved, but they had just stood staring at him and had not replied. He had made a plea to his guide in spirit to help him, but there had been nothing but complete silence.

After a minute or two the two spirit forms had gradually disappeared, but Simon said he was left feeling distinctly upset and quite scared.

I suggested that I call at his house once more.

'I think you better had, since you started this!' he told me.

Once again I found it strange that a person who was not only following a spiritual pathway but who was also purporting to be a developing medium would speak in this manner.

That afternoon when I arrived back at the house I was surprised to see an ashen-faced Simon opening the door. He was looking even more agitated and nervous than he had been the previous day. I told him that I would like to attempt communication with the two spirit ladies and he agreed to this.

We both sat together quietly for a few moments. Gradually I became aware of the spirit presence of the two ladies I had seen the day before.

Gladys spoke first. She told me that it was her side of the family that had the psychic gifts that had been passed down to Simon and Claire. Whilst Claire had been living her physical life she had behaved properly and used her gifts responsibly. It was since she had passed on to the spirit world that she had noticed that her brother Simon was not using his in a responsible manner at all, but was doing things that could potentially harm other people – the very people he was supposed to be helping.

I turned to Simon and asked if he could hear or see the ladies in spirit. He told me that he could see the outline of two women in spirit form but could not hear anything at all.

Gladys began to speak once more. She told me that she was Simon and Claire's grandmother on their mother's side and that she had passed to the spirit world when Simon was only eight years of age. She said that she was very worried about her grandson, as although he had psychic gifts and the potential to become a very good medium he had not reached that stage of his development just yet. Claire had been much further advanced and unfortunately this had caused Simon to be quite jealous of her. She had always tried to instil into Simon that he should not attempt to undertake psychic readings for people until he was ready and able to do so. Since her tragic passing, however, Simon had taken it upon himself to offer private readings and unfortunately, because he was not really ready to do so, he was upsetting many people. The things he had been telling them were making them unhappy and afraid.

I looked at Simon. I could see that he was nervous about what I was about to say. He knew that his sister Claire had been telling me the truth about the situation and he was terribly ashamed. I felt sorry for the man because I knew that in reality he was sincere in his wish to help people, but that he had taken the gift he had and misused it rather than waiting until he was fully developed and truly able to help people as mediums should. He was aware of his sister's warnings but had chosen not to heed them and had suffered as a result. His guilty conscience and resentment of Claire's gifts had brought about the nightmare state where he saw his beloved sister's face change from beauty into ugliness. When Claire had passed on to the spirit world he had thought that he would be able to take over her mantle and receive the adulation that she had received as a particularly gifted medium, but he had achieved none of these things.

I told Simon that for some people it takes a long, long time to develop as a medium. His sister was extraordinary in that she was so naturally developed that I felt she would have been capable of passing on messages from the spirit world as a small child. Simon agreed that that had indeed been the case and said that he had felt terribly jealous of the interest people took in his sister because of the wise words and eye-opening details she had uttered as a young girl. He had wanted people to pay attention to him in the same way and had felt left out and undervalued.

I could understand in a small way how Simon had felt. I knew that my own brother had felt rather pushed out when my grandmother had paid more attention to me because she knew that I had been chosen to follow in her mediumistic footsteps. As a child I had been rather awful and I can remember revelling in the attention I received whilst watching my brother standing on the sidelines. My brother has told me that he almost hated me at those times because he felt that I was more loved than he was. This of course was not the case, but looking at the situation through a child's eyes I could well understand it. The trouble with Simon was that he had not dropped those feelings but had carried them through into his adult life and when his sister had passed on to the spirit world he had felt that he could capture some of that love for himself.

I knew that Simon had the ability to become a very good instrument for spirit if he would only buckle down, attend development classes and take things slowly. I explained to him that it was not meant for him to rush out and attempt to conduct sittings for people yet, as he was just not ready. He was doing more harm than good and eventually, if he continued, would have a huge karmic debt to repay. But he had great potential and could develop into an outstanding medium if only he would take my advice and the advice of his sister in spirit.

Thankfully Simon listened both to me and to Claire. Today he is continuing with his development as a medium and I have heard wonderful reports from the head of the circle he joined. One day it is expected that Simon will be equally as good, if not a better medium than his sister Claire and will be able to help a great many people.

CHAPTER 11

A Joint Message

It sometimes happens that two people receive similar warnings from spirit when they are about to undergo an experience or do something as simple as taking a trip out together. My wife Gwen and I often turn to one another before carrying out plans to do something or go somewhere and say 'Nah!' at the last minute. Although Gwen would say she is not in the least bit psychic, I know that she has great intuition and the spirit people work through her in this way. If she makes a comment about something we plan to do which would radically change those plans, I do tend to listen to her. If I don't, on more than one occasion it has been to my cost.

There have also been occasions when I have been considering doing something or going somewhere but my own inner voice has whispered, 'No!' On checking with my spirit guide Sam, I have been told that the course of action I was considering was not best for me. Moments later Gwen may come up and tell me that she has been thinking about the situation and her conclusion will be more or less the same as what I have just been told by my guide. Whether she knows it or not, Sam is very good at communicating with my wife, even though she is neither clairvoyant nor clairaudient.

In certain situations people in the world of spirit may be desperate to alter the course of events for their loved ones here in the physical world. They can see something is about to happen that is not meant to be on their pathway and so they do their best to alter the course of events. The people they influence may well not be aware of what is happening at the time, but after the event it is obviously clear that 'divine intervention' has taken place.

John wrote to tell me about something he had experienced in his childhood. He told me that he was not a great believer in the afterlife but by the same token did not actually disbelieve. The events that took place on 11 May 1985, when he was nine years of age, however, must have given him food for thought.

John told me that on that morning he had played football for his local junior team. In the afternoon he was being taken by his father and grandfather to watch the real thing when Bradford City played Lincoln City at the Bradford City football stadium at Valley Parade. John's grandfather, Eddie, had played for Bradford City in his younger years and it was to be quite an event that day as Bradford City were to parade the old Third Division championship trophy round the ground prior to kick-off. All three were very excited at the prospect and John felt very proud that his granddad had once played for Bradford City.

It had been arranged that John and his father would collect his grandfather at 1 o'clock from his house in Bradford, which was about eight miles from their own home. They would then proceed to the game.

John's mother wrapped him up to protect him against the Yorkshire chill and accompanied him to the car where his father was waiting. But just as John reached out for the door handle he burst into tears and told his dad that he just could not get into the car.

'Needless to say,' he told me, 'my dad told me to stop being silly and get into the car.'

In spite of what his father was telling him, however, John just could not open the door to the car. He felt that someone – he did not know who – was telling him in his head that he should not go to the football match. He could not control his crying and felt quite embarrassed. In spite of cajoling from both his mother and father, nothing changed his mind. He just could not get into that car.

John's father telephoned his grandfather and told him, 'The silly little bugger won't get in the car! I've never seen anything like it! He's just crying and won't get in.'

'Granddad was upset,' John told me, 'but for some reason, although he had been looking forward to going to the game and had been offered an alternative lift to the ground, he declined, as he had begun to feel unwell, even though prior to my dad's phone call he had been ready and excited to be going to the match.'

John's father did not speak to him for the rest of the afternoon and made it quite clear that John had ruined his chance to see the trophy being paraded around the football ground.

In an attempt to calm things down and get John's father talking to him again, John's mother decided that she would cook an early meal. It was at approximately 3.30 in the afternoon, as his mother called him through for his meal, that John happened to look through the lounge window. In the distance he could see faint black smoke.

'Something's going on somewhere!' said John's father.

John replied, 'It's Valley Parade and it's on fire!'

This brought a great frown of condemnation onto his father's face, as he thought that John was making a very lame excuse for making him miss his football match.

Within five minutes the telephone rang. To get away from his father's searing glances, John leaped from his chair and ran to answer it. He told me, 'Without me even speaking to give the phone number or to utter a word, a voice came down the other end of the phone who instinctively knew it was me answering, even though there was my mum, dad, four sisters and me in the house. "You felt it too then," the voice said. It was my grand-dad!'

On 11 May 1985, 56 people, many of them children, never returned from that supposedly joyous afternoon at the football match.

John says that he and his grandfather never ever spoke of their conversation on the telephone that day, nor did they mention it to any members of their family. In 1990 John's grandfather passed on to the spirit world. After the funeral John's frail grandmother took him to one side and told him, 'Just before the pain got too much, Eddie wanted you to know that Brian had said that it wasn't your time. There would be more trophies to see, but not this one.'

'She wanted to know what the message was all about,' John told me, 'but I just couldn't tell her or anyone.'

The Brian that his grandfather had spoken about was an uncle to John. He had been UK table tennis champion but unfortunately had passed on to the spirit world as the result of a heart attack during an exhibition when he was just 27 years of age. John had never met his uncle in his physical life, but had seen a photograph of him which was kept in a silver frame at his grandparents' house. He had always been transfixed by that photograph and had often wondered what his Uncle Brian was like and what he would think of his nephew. He says that he can feel his uncle's presence all around him and has even thought that he has heard his voice.

I am quite sure that it was 'Uncle Brian' who came to both John and his grandfather on that fateful Saturday. He saved both of them by first impressing the young John with a distinct desire *not* to go to the football match and then by speaking to his father. It was indeed not their time!

Katie told me of an experience where both she and another member of her family received messages that would ultimately prevent an untimely passing.

Katie was in the estate agency office where she worked in a small town just outside Leeds, but she had nearly not gone into work at all. She had had a niggling feeling that something was wrong all the previous night and in fact it had got so bad in the morning that she had almost decided not go into work that day. She had mentioned her feelings of dread to her mother, with whom she lived, but she had told her that she was being silly and to get off to work and not worry.

As Katie sat at her desk, though, she just could not settle. If anything, the feelings were getting worse. She just knew that something was wrong and she began to feel more and more certain that there was a problem at home. She tried telephoning her mother, but was unable to get an answer. At last, not being able to stand it any longer, she asked her manager whether she could take an early lunch break, as she felt that there might be a problem with her mother, who suffered from diabetes. Her manager agreed and Katie raced home as fast as she possibly could.

As she parked her car in front of her home she was surprised to see her brother Mike's car already there. Mike never called at his mother's house during the daytime, but there he was standing on the doorstep alternately hammering on the door and shouting, 'Mum!' through the letterbox. He did not have a key to his mother's house because he no longer lived there, having married two years previously. As soon as Katie arrived, he grabbed her front door key off her, opened the door and raced through to the kitchen. Their mother was lying there on the floor. Mike and Katie recognized that she had lapsed into a diabetic coma.

Katie called an ambulance and she and her brother carried their mother through to a sofa in the sitting room whilst they waited for the ambulance to arrive. Not many minutes later Mike was showing the paramedics through the door and their mother was whisked off to the local hospital where, I am pleased to report, she made a full recovery.

'It was very strange that day,' Katie told me. 'Whilst Mike and I were sitting in the hospital and everybody was looking after Mum, he told me that he hadn't been able to settle at all the previous night and, just like me, had had a niggling feeling that something was wrong. He had also felt as I had done – he had known that the "something wrong" involved Mum. He can't afford to just take time off work, but once he got into work he just couldn't settle and had to get to see her. Mum and I have lived on our own since Dad died three years ago. Dad always used to worry terribly about Mum's diabetes because he knew that on odd occasions she would be late in giving herself the medication she needed. I always reminded her every morning about it and she'd always say that she was going to do it right then, but that morning she must have forgotten. D'you think it was Dad telling Mike and me that Mum was in trouble? D'you think that he knew that she was going to forget her medication and that she'd end up being really ill?'

I told Katie that I was positive that her father had impressed both of his children to get to their mother as quickly as they possibly could. I was also positive that he had indeed foreseen possibly fatal consequences and had been trying desperately to get a message through to either Katie or Mike so that their mother would not be left alone that morning. Thank goodness he succeeded!

CHAPTER 12

The Touch of an Angel

It feels like the most natural thing in the world – a gentle hand stroking your hair or touching your cheek when you feel that life has thrown so many injustices at you that you just cannot take any more. When you feel so down that you just do not know what you are going to do next, the comforting feeling of an unseen hand taking yours or the gentle pressure of a sympathetic arm on your shoulder can make all the difference in the world.

We may not understand it and we may not always think about it, but the people in the spirit world are always around us. They oversee our lives. They feel for us when we are down, and in exactly the same way that they would have done when they were here in their physical lives, they give solace where they can. This often comes in the form of the gentle touch of a hand pressing against us.

I am a tactile person and have no problem at all with throwing my arms around somebody to give them a hug, but not everybody is the same. I have been asked, 'How can my grandpa be putting his arm around me when he was just not the sort of person who would have done that when he was here?' The answer to that question is that when a person passes over to the world of spirit, their personality still remains the same, but generally their social 'programming' no longer has any effect. We humans are generally gregarious and friendly. We like to be with people, and when somebody is feeling down it is a natural reaction to reach out to them and pat their hand or put an arm around them. It is only our earthly programming which prevents this. The people in the spirit world are no different. When they see a loved one in the depths of despair or worrying over a situation, they will draw close and give as much physical comfort as they possibly can.

Recently I was talking to a young lady whom I shall name Lisa. She was telling me about an experience she had had only a couple of weeks prior to our conversation.

Lisa explained that she had often used public transport whilst travelling around the city where she worked. One day as she was climbing onto a bus she slipped and fell out of the bus and onto the pavement. Although she was unhurt, she felt shocked and terribly embarrassed as she picked herself up from the floor. With quaking knees she proceeded to walk back to her flat to change her now dirty clothes. As she was walking along she clearly felt the pressure of a hand on her shoulder. She looked around, but there was nobody close to her.

'Was it my guardian angel, Derek?' she asked me.

I was able to tell her that it was most definitely a loved one from the world of spirit placing a hand of reassurance on her shoulder.

It is not unusual to feel a comforting hand stroking your hair or pressing your arm or shoulder at times of stress and emotional upset.

Mandy wrote to me to tell me about her experience. She began by saying that her story was not a fantastic one, nor was it a life-saving one, but to her it made all the difference in the world.

As a young child Mandy had been abused both mentally and physically. These events left her unable to trust people and suffering nightmares almost every night. In due course she married and had two children, and she now feels safe and loved, but unfortunately the nightmares still occur. Sometimes she will wake up terrified that something is going to happen to her and her young son and daughter.

One night Mandy had gone to bed early but woken up shaking and crying from a nightmare. As she woke, she could feel a hand stroking her hair. Thinking it was her husband, she turned over, but realized that he was not there as he had not yet come to bed. She could still feel the pressure of a hand gently stroking her hair and although she did not feel afraid and instinctively knew that what she was feeling was 'not of this world', she felt a little unnerved and quietly thanked the presence but asked it to 'please go away'. Immediately she felt the hand leave her hair and she lay down once more. Though she did not sleep much for the rest of that night, she knew in her heart that something or somebody had been watching over her and was trying to comfort her.

Mandy finished by telling me that though what had happened was not a miracle, it was special to her in that it made her feel the most safe and comforted she had felt since she was a very small child.

Yet another instance when a comforting hand was felt at a time of great distress comes from Helen.

When Helen was 23 years old, her daughter Lauren was born. There were complications that resulted in her giving birth two weeks early by artificial means within a hospital setting. Whilst she was in labour, a further series of complications occurred which caused Lauren to stop breathing when she was born and she had to be resuscitated.

Within 24 hours of Lauren's birth the doctors advised Helen to call her family and a priest for spiritual support, as they did not feel that Lauren would make it. Helen was not allowed to stay at the hospital with her daughter and was sent home, but within 15 minutes of arriving at her house she received a telephone call from a nurse telling her that her daughter had been airlifted to a sick children's hospital as the hospital in which she had been born felt that there was nothing more that they could do for her.

When Helen arrived at Lauren's bedside she found she had been placed on life support. She told me that when she saw her daughter her legs went numb and she fell to her knees. 'All I could do was pray to God, "Please take me instead. My daughter chose to be here! Please give her a life and take me instead!"'

A few days passed and Lauren was not improving. She was still on a life-support machine which was breathing for her. The worst was feared. Helen and her husband were sitting in vigil by their baby's bed. 'I was not going to give up hope,' Helen said. 'I called her my sunshine and sang the song "You are my Sunshine" to her every day.'

On the fourth day of Lauren's fight for life Helen was sitting in her usual spot beside her bed, her husband was sitting at the end of the bed and Helen was praying harder than she had ever prayed in her life before. She was imagining how she could watch over her daughter from the other side if only God would take her instead.

'Somebody must have heard my prayers and listened to my thoughts,' she told me, 'because all of a sudden I felt a hand squeeze my right shoulder. It was such a strong squeeze and such a cold feeling ran down my right side that the first thing I did was look to see who it was. There was no one there, so my next reaction was to check to see if a window was open.'

There was no window open. Helen asked her husband whether he had felt the cold and in response he had pointed out that they were both sitting under the heat lamp positioned over Lauren's bed.

Then for a second time Helen felt a gentle squeeze on her right shoulder and a feeling of peace which she tells me she just cannot put into words. 'I felt so completely relaxed and felt so loved – like God or someone was surrounding me with love.'

It was at this exact moment that Helen and her husband noticed that Lauren had started breathing. They just could not believe it, yet at the same time Helen says that she knew without doubt that her baby girl was going to be alright. 'It was as though she had been given the strength and the spark of life to make it, Derek,' she told me. She whispered in her baby's ear, 'Not only are you my angel, but we are surrounded by angels. God has sent us an angel. Keep fighting, sweetheart, and let the angels help you!'

Lauren came home on Christmas Eve, exactly 11 days after her birth. Helen tells me that she knows from the bottom of her heart that God had sent her an angel of healing to help her daughter and to give them both the courage and strength to see things through.

Lauren is now a beautiful girl of eight who shows no sign of ever being so ill. The doctors cannot explain the quick change in her condition as a baby, but Helen can! She will always remember the day when an angel came to help her and her family and will always be grateful for the gift of life for herself and her daughter.

Dylan was only nine months old when he started having febrile convulsions. Every time he was unwell strange things would happen – doors would open and close and the television would turn itself on and off.

Paula, Dylan's mother, remembers one particularly bad night when Dylan had just returned from the hospital following a convulsion. He was approximately two years of age at the time and was suffering a throat infection. Paula recalls that he just would not stop crying. She was in the bedroom trying to comfort him when suddenly the door opened wide and then after a few moments shut again. After that Dylan stopped crying and went to sleep. The next day he said that his mother's nan had come to see him and had stroked his hair, saying, 'It's OK, Dylan. Don't cry. Go to sleep.'

Paula tells me that Dylan had never met her grandmother, but that they did have a photograph of her in the living room and consequently he would have been aware of who she was.

Since that day Paula has often watched her son playing with his toys and chattering away. When she has asked who he is talking to, the reply is always: 'It's Nanny!' In Paula's own words:

'It has given me great comfort to know that my nan is still around me and my son, watching over us. Dylan has been clear of the convulsions now for nearly a year and he has not spoken of my nan for some time now, but when strange things start to happen, I know

it's her way of telling me she is with us. My son has no fear of death now, which sometimes can be a problem. I will tell him not to run across the road because he will get hurt or killed and his answer to me is: "It will be OK, Mummy, because if that happens I will come back to see you and will still be here." I have told him not everybody can see people who have died and that he is special.'

Laura feels that she was not only touched by an angelic being but actually saw her.

Things had not been going very well for Laura. She was working two jobs to make ends meet and was emotional and exhausted most of the time.

One day she had come home from her morning job and had flopped down onto the sofa before getting ready for her evening job as a waitress. Feeling tired, she decided to lie down on her bed for a short while. She says that she can remember lying there feeling overwhelmed and trying not to give in to tears because she was so unhappy.

Whilst she was resting with her eyes closed, she felt a gentle hand stroking her cheek. She quickly opened her eyes and for a brief moment glimpsed the face of a woman standing over her. She immediately disappeared and

Laura noticed something white flutter very quickly up towards the ceiling of her room and disappear as well.

Laura did not understand what had happened, but she told me that she felt much more light-hearted and able to cope with her life after the visitation.

Many, many more people have been touched by a comforting hand at times of great stress and anxiety. When times are hard and you feel that you have nowhere to turn and nobody to help you, remember that out there, beyond our physical world, there are angelic beings guarding us. The next time you are feeling down or something is bothering you, look out for the impression of a gentle hand pressing lightly on the top of your head or maybe quickly brushing your hair. Maybe there will be a slight pressure on your arm or shoulder. You can be sure that it is somebody from the world of spirit who has come to give you comfort and solace in your time of need.

CHAPTER 13

The Reunion

Most of the people I met during the time I was conducting private sittings at my office in Liverpool would come back time and time again and over the years they became friends. Mothers would bring their daughters and sons, sometimes their husbands, and on regular occasions would turn up with their own mothers, whom they had told about me and who now wanted a sitting.

One such person was Esther, who used to travel to Liverpool every year with her daughter Lucy from their home in Cumbria. Esther was a real character and used to spend the first ten minutes or so of our meeting regaling me with tales of what her husband Donald had been up to during the months since I had last seen her.

It was with great sadness that I learned of Esther's illness and passing to the spirit world when Lucy came to visit me in late 1998. Lucy was devoted to her mother and had spent many weeks caring for her.

'I had a very strange experience just prior to my mother passing to spirit, Derek,' she said, 'and I wondered whether you could explain to me what it was.'

Lucy told me that at about 4 a.m. one morning she had woken to the smell of flowers in her bedroom. At the side of her bed there was a very well-defined mist. It did not form a human shape, but Lucy just knew that there was someone in her room in visitation. She told me that she felt very peaceful and comforted. The mist gradually moved towards the wall which separated Lucy's bedroom from her mother's and disappeared.

Lucy rose at about 5.30 a.m. and went through to her mother's room, where she found Esther sitting up in bed looking very calm. She told Lucy that she was having some trouble breathing and asked her to go and get Donald, who was sleeping in another bedroom, as she felt it was time to go to hospital.

Lucy and Donald took Esther to hospital and after examining her the doctor immediately admitted her. Both Lucy and Donald knew that time was short. Esther chatted with them for a while before falling asleep. Whilst she was asleep Donald left the room to find a tea-vending machine. Whilst he was away, Esther woke up very briefly and asked Lucy to take care of her father before promptly going back to sleep once more. A few moments later she ceased breathing. She was gone! Lucy told me that she felt that her mother had chosen the moment whilst Donald was away from her side because she knew that if she died in his presence he would just break down. 'He did, anyway,' she added. 'They had been married for almost 50 years!'

Lucy had a question for me: 'Can you tell me what the mist was at the side of the bed and why I woke up to the smell of flowers, Derek?'

I gladly explained to her that what she had experienced was Esther's mother, her maternal grandmother, coming to assist her daughter in her transition over to the world of spirit. She had come in visitation to Lucy to let her know that it was nearly time for Esther to leave the physical world and that she would be caring for her just as Lucy had done. She had also come to imbue Lucy with a sense of peace, calm and acceptance and to reassure her that she was not losing her mother, it was just that they were being separated for a short time.

'That would explain what happened a few months later then,' Lucy told me.

It was only four short months after Esther had passed over that Donald started to feel unwell. He was admitted to hospital but was told that the prognosis was not good: he was suffering from terminal cancer. He spent his last weeks in a hospice where Lucy visited him every day. They both knew that his time was drawing very close and one day at about 7 a.m., whilst Donald was still asleep, Lucy went over to the washbasin in his room to rinse her hands. As she looked up, she saw reflected in the mirror over the basin a mist floating about her father's bed, similar to that which she had seen just prior to her mother's passing to the spirit world. Lucy just knew that it was her mother, 'just as I had felt that it was a spirit presence standing next to my bed just before Mum died'.

As the mist continued to drift around Donald's bed he woke and smiled. 'It was the most beautiful smile,' said Lucy, 'and then he was gone!'

Esther had come to collect her beloved husband and help him on his journey over to the world of spirit.

Later that day Lucy spoke to a nurse at the hospice and told her what she had seen. The nurse said that the staff at the hospice were quite used to seeing things like that. She added that it was not uncommon to see former patients either. They were generally very happy and just wanted the staff who had cared for them during the final days of their physical lives to know that. 'Working in a hospice would certainly turn many sceptics into believers,' the nurse told Lucy.

I have had a similar experience myself. I was sitting with my own father one day when his time to pass to the spirit world was drawing close. He had become so weak by this time that his bed had been brought down into the sitting room.

My mother was in hospital with pneumonia at the time and was very ill. My dad was very worried about her, in spite of the appalling illness he was suffering himself. I knew that his time was measured in hours rather than days, and he had reached the point where even speaking had become an effort, but he would continue to ask after my mother and make sure that somebody was with her and that she had everything that she needed.

Now the effort of trying to speak had exhausted him and he was lying back with his head propped up on a pillow. Suddenly I noticed the expression on his face change. He looked as though he was meeting somebody that he had not seen for a very long time.

'Mum,' he shouted, 'is that you?'

My paternal grandmother had passed on to the spirit world when my father was a young boy and he had been left in the care of his father and his older sisters. I glanced towards the end of the bed and sure enough, I could see the hazy outline of a woman in spirit form. I recognized her from the photographs I had seen of my grandmother in the family album.

As I continued to look at her she was joined by three or four more spirit people, all smiling and looking joyous. I instantly recognized my grandfather as I had known him during my childhood, and this was confirmed by my father, who suddenly cried out, 'Dad! I'm sorry, Dad! I'm sorry I didn't make it to your funeral!' The emotion in his voice was heartbreaking and I felt quite upset for him, as I did not know to what he was referring.

'And there's Julia,' my father continued, as he recognized his sister who had passed on to the spirit world before him. His expression was incredulous. He had not really ever believed in the spirit world and had always scoffed at my work and referred to it as 'messing about with those bloody ghosts'.

The shadowy outlines faded and my father dropped his head back once more onto the pillow. 'Did you see them, lad?' he asked me.

'Yes, Dad, I saw them,' I told him.

Though nothing was said at that time, I know that my father had at last accepted that there was a world beyond this physical one and that his family was waiting for him to join them.

The following day he passed on to the world of spirit. I have no doubt whatsoever that my grandmother, my grandfather and my aunts were there waiting for him with open arms.

When I visited my devastated and still very ill mother in hospital she asked about the final hours that I had spent with Dad. I told her what I had seen and about his words of apology to his father.

'Oh yes, I remember that well,' Mum said. 'Your dad was away at sea when your granddad died and he never forgave himself for not being able to get home to go to his funeral. We didn't have the money though, Degs. We couldn't afford to have him fly home, not with six kids to look after. Your dad felt terribly guilty, though.'

I did not know until that time of the burden of guilt that my father had carried with him over the years. If only he had opened up to me and discussed the situation I would have been able to tell him that he should shed his feelings of guilt, as his father was now in the spirit world and he would understand how difficult it would have been for his son to travel the thousands of miles to attend his funeral.

Chapter 14

Reincarnation

It has always been my belief and my truth that we all reincarnate a number of times, returning to this physical world over and again during our own personal process of soul growth. I have also come into contact with several people who have some recall of a previous life. Many more people have told me that they have a certain 'feeling' for a particular time in history. Some of these people feel that their past lies in a distant land, whereas others are firmly convinced that they have lived in this country before but in a different era. Occasionally a person may feel drawn to more than one era. In these cases, they are recalling experiences from more than one incarnation.

Some years ago, during my early days with Granada Breeze's *Psychic Livetime*, I had a friend who was a hugely popular master hypnotist. His name was Alan Bates. At that time he was appearing at venues throughout the country with his comedy hypnotist routine.

One day I was talking to Alan about the more serious elements of hypnotism, particularly hypnotic regression. I don't know how the idea came about, but we decided that we might just be able to complement each another in a stage show. *The Paranormal Experience* was born!

The show consisted of a demonstration of mediumship followed by a light-hearted hypnosis routine. The third element was the part that people were to find most fascinating. Members of the audience would be asked if they would like to volunteer to take part in a demonstration of hypnotic regression. Once a person had been regressed by Alan, I would then use my mediumistic skills to talk to them in their regressed state. We achieved some amazing results.

William lived near Chester, had heard about *The Paranormal Experience* and wanted to take part in the show. He agreed to be put into a hypnotic state by Alan and be regressed to an earlier life.

As William drifted back down the years to a time far beyond his present lifetime under the watchful eye of

Alan, he suddenly opened his eyes. He had reached a previous lifetime. He was not in this country but in Germany approximately 150 years ago. It was at this point that I stepped forward and began speaking to him.

William told me that he was a young man and a member of quite a large family, having a number of sisters and brothers. I talked to him about his mother, who found it quite difficult trying to feed such a large brood, and about his father, who was unable to work due to a chest complaint. In his hypnotically regressed state, William agreed that his mother had great difficulty in finding enough food for the family and that his father was a very weak man who suffered with great pain in his chest.

I also spoke with the regressed William about his work as an apprentice to a leather worker and how difficult he found it in the cold winter days working with his hands in the freezing weather. William agreed and seemed comforted by the fact that I was able to tell him that his two brothers would very soon find work for themselves and this would ease the dire financial straits that the family found themselves in.

William thanked me and seemed to drift off to sleep. At that point Alan signalled to me that I should cease talking to him so that he could bring him forward to the present day and his present lifetime.

William was amazed when people related to him what had happened. 'I've always had a feeling that I had some connection with Germany,' he said. 'I've never been there and I don't have any family links there at all, but I've always felt that the country was familiar in some way.'

There were many such occurrences where people were regressed to a previous time. There was the young lady who had spent a previous life in the Scottish isles as a lonely only child to a couple who scratched out a living in a croft. A young man was quite embarrassed to find out that in a previous life he had been a young lady in Elizabethan England. An older lady was regressed to Victorian times, where she was a scullery maid in a large house in London. Another girl was a 'flapper' in the roaring twenties. All were excited and amazed at the proof that they had indeed been here before.

It was obvious from the diversity of the regressions that there was no pattern to people's returns to this world. For some people their last lifetime was just a few years before their birth, whereas others would go back hundreds and hundreds of years. This did not surprise me. As I have said before, it is up to us when we return to the Earth plane. We may choose to do it within a few years of our passing to the spirit world or we may decide to spend a while in the world beyond before undertaking the rigours of a physical life once more.

One reincarnation experience that touched me had nothing at all to do with my work with Alan but concerned a young man named Sean who visited me at my office in Liverpool. He was in his mid-twenties and was a cheerful sort normally, but at the time of his visit to me he was rather anxious. He was happily married with a young son and had a good job working as a manager in a local DIY store.

Sean told me that for as long as he could remember he had felt that he belonged in another time. He said that he had constant dreams of living in London in the late 1800s. These dreams were really vivid. He could tell me all about his family – his mother Ethel and his father Alf and his younger sisters and older brother. 'I even know that my name was Daniel,' he told me.

Sean recollected working with his father Alf as a coster-monger in the mean Victorian streets and although he said that he felt that his life had not been an easy one, he did not feel that he had suffered greatly as he had a home to go to at night and a loving family around him. Even if food was a little short at times, they managed to struggle through and were better off than many of the families who lived and worked around their area. When he was 21 he had met and married a local girl and they had had a couple of children.

'It wouldn't be so bad if it was only dreams, Derek,' he said, 'but even when I'm awake I sometimes go into a daydream and there I am, back in London all those years ago! I think I must be going mad! And the worst of it is, although I can tell you everything about my life in those times up to the age of 26, beyond that time everything is a blank. Do you think this is a sign that I'm going to die? I'm 25 now and I'm feeling a bit afraid!'

Sean's experience was a classic example of somebody who has recall of a previous incarnation. I was able to reassure him that he was not going mad at all. I also told him that he was definitely not due to pass over to the world of spirit for a very long time. I explained to him that it is our destiny to experience everything in order to achieve soul growth and ultimately reach a situation where we cease to incarnate into earthly lives. So what had happened in the last lifetime would not be repeated in this lifetime. If we pass over to the spirit world at a young age in one lifetime, in another life we will live to a great age. If we suffer hardship once, on our return we will be given the opportunity to experience an easier lifestyle.

Sean breathed a sigh of relief. 'So I'm not about to pop my clogs then?'

'No,' I told him with a smile.

It was a more light-hearted and enlightened Sean who walked out of my office that afternoon.

Sean's experience is unusual but not unknown. I have heard reports of people who can give such detailed information of events in a previous lifetime that it has been possible to check and confirm that what they have said is correct.

The experiences of people like Sean and my time working with Alan Bates have confirmed to me that what my guide Sam has told me is correct: that no matter how long it takes, we all do return to Earth in order to achieve soul growth.

CHAPTER 15

Children and Visitation

My own first meeting with a spirit from the higher side of life is well documented. At the age of six I was living with my mother and my elder brother and sister at the home of my grandmother in Bootle, Liverpool. My father worked as a merchant seaman and was away from home for very long periods of time. My grandmother's house was a large three-storey Victorian one close to the port of Liverpool. Every day after school we three children would go to the top of the house to play whilst our evening meal was being prepared.

One day we were called downstairs for our tea. Being the youngest, I was always trailing in the wake of my brother and sister and was the last to arrive at the table.

On this day, however, I was brought to a halt on the first landing of the house by the sight of a man I did not recognize. He reached out towards me and I had the distinct feeling that he had ruffled my hair. To me, he was as tangible as my mother and grandmother, who were at that time in the kitchen, so I was afraid. I thought there was a stranger in the house. After staring wide-eyed at the man, I continued on my way down the stairs. Never had I reached the ground floor more quickly!

I ran into the kitchen in a state of fear. 'There's a strange man on the landing!' I cried as I threw myself into my mother's arms. Putting me to one side, she ran quickly to the stairway, followed by my gran. I heard them running up the stairs to the first landing and doors being opened and slammed shut. After a few moments they returned. They couldn't find any stranger. There was no man lurking in the doorways of the first landing.

Gran asked me to describe the man that I had seen. Then she took out a photograph from a tin box she kept on the shelf in the kitchen. 'Is this the man you saw?' she asked me.

'That's him! That's the man!' I cried, pointing at the photograph of a man wearing a long dark overcoat and a flat cap.

Gran looked at my mother with a knowing expression on her face. 'I knew it!' she said.

It was this point that my grandmother realized that I would be the next member of our family to follow in her footsteps as a medium. The man I had seen on the stairs was my grandfather, my grandmother's first husband, who had passed on to the spirit world a few years before my birth.

A child seeing the spirit form of a passed loved one does not, of course, always indicate that that child will grow up to become a medium, as it is not always on that child's pathway to do so. There are, however, many recordings of children being aware of people from the spirit world. Their minds are uncrowded and uncluttered by the problems we all experience as we grow and take on daily life in the material world.

It is not unknown for a young child to have an 'imaginary friend', i.e. the spirit of a person, usually but not always another child, or even an animal, who accompanies them through their early years. I know of families who have been driven to distraction by having to cater for this 'friend' they cannot see. These beings, however, are not figments of the child's imagination but are spirits in visitation – sometimes constantly – and will remain so until the child grows and matures, sometimes right up to puberty.

Ella had a friend from the spirit world. He was a boy of about the same age who was named Mickey. Mickey went everywhere with Ella. He had his own chair and his own place at the dinner table. Ella's family grew quite used to having Mickey around and she tells me that there were a number of occasions during her childhood when she felt that Mickey had saved her from harm or injury.

As is the case with all spirit friends, Mickey faded from Ella's life as she grew older. By the time she had reached her teenage years she had forgotten all about him. It was only when she reached her twenties and felt drawn to the world of Spiritualism that she started to think once more about Mickey and remember their experiences as childhood friends.

Ella received many messages from mediums at the churches telling her that she should develop as a medium herself. Finally, she found herself a place in a development circle and came on in leaps and bounds.

During one gathering, the presiding medium turned to Ella and said, 'I've a young chap here who tells me that he's known you for a long time. He has been designated to remain by your side as your guide. His name is Mickey!'

Ella was astounded. All the time she had played with her little spirit friend she had not known that one day he would be her spirit guide.

* * *

A child's mind is so open and clear. Children are not born with the concept of good and evil, it is people in the physical world who instil these things into their mind. From the moment of our birth we all have experiences both good and bad, and these experiences are all preordained and part of our pathway.

Sometimes when children are ill and have a high temperature they may start to 'hallucinate', as the medical profession calls it, and see beings who frighten them. They are not hallucinating at all. What they are seeing is spirit beings who are unfamiliar to them and so they are frightened, just as I was frightened as a six-year-old boy when I saw the spirit form of my grandfather in my grandmother's house.

I can recall Gwen telling me of a time when her daughter Jaynie was ill and had a very high temperature. Jaynie was only four years old at the time. She had been put to bed but had woken up screaming. Gwen rushed up the stairs and opened the bedroom door to see Jaynie sitting up pointing towards the end of the bed and insisting through her sobs that there was an old man sitting there. Gwen could see nothing and tried to reassure her daughter that she was safe and that there was nobody in the room. Jaynie, however, would not settle and kept insisting to her mother that there was indeed an old man sitting on the end of her bed. In the end she had to be taken to another bedroom where she calmed down and went to sleep for the night.

When Gwen told me this story I asked her whether she knew anything about the history of the house she had been living in at the time. She was able to tell me that it was at that time about 100 years old and had been empty for a couple of years before she moved in because the previous owner, an old man, had passed on to the spirit world and the house had needed some work doing to it. Consequently it had taken quite a while to be sold.

Although I did not know the house and I had not been a visitor to it, I was able to explain that it was more than likely that the man Jaynie had seen sitting on the end of her bed was the previous owner who had returned in visitation to his old home.

Some children see people from the spirit world who are familiar to them. A grandmother or grandfather, for example, may come in visitation to their beloved grandchild. That child may see their grandparent in spirit form and be excited and point, insisting that 'Nana' or 'Gaga' is in the room. They are not afraid because the spirits appear to them as they remember them in their physical form.

Samantha tells me that her son Leon was not in the best of health as a small child as he suffered from asthma. If Samantha was out of the room when he had a problem, his sister Maisy would run to her and alert her. One day Maisy came running to Samantha shouting, 'Mummy! Mummy! The lady said go to Leon!' When Samantha reached the room she could see that Leon needed medical attention.

Samantha says that her two nephews have also seen a lady when they have been unwell, but who she was remained a mystery until one day the photograph album was brought out. Maisy and her two cousins were there at the time. To everybody's surprise when they saw the photograph of Samantha's grandmother they shouted out, 'That's the old lady that looks after us when we're poorly!'

Samantha explains that none of the children have ever seen her own grandmother because she passed to spirit when Samantha, who was her eldest grandchild, was 14 years of age.

Samantha makes the comment that she had never given anything like angels or spirits a thought up to that time but ever since the incident with the photograph and the children she has derived a lot of comfort from the knowledge that whenever anyone close to her passes to spirit, they will be back to visit her one day.

* * *

After the breakdown of her marriage, Hilary returned with her two children to live with her father in her childhood home. She was absolutely devastated when he passed unexpectedly on to the world of spirit. She tried to explain to her two children, Sonia aged six and Jamie aged three, that Granddad had had to leave them to go and live with the angels. The two children, especially Jamie, were inconsolable, as they loved their granddad. Jamie would cry for him persistently and would not accept it when he was told that his granddad was no longer there.

A month or two passed and Hilary became more and more worried about her small son. He moped around and cried a lot and asked for his grandfather all the time. Hilary was at her wits' end. She took Jamie to visit the doctor, but all he could suggest was some medicine to calm him down at bedtime.

Late one afternoon Hilary was at home watching television. Sonia was in her bedroom and Jamie was playing with some toys in the corner of the room about ten feet away from where Hilary was sitting. Above the sound of the television, Hilary suddenly became aware that her son was talking to somebody. She could not see anybody, but he was having a definite conversation. She called out his name. He turned to look at her and said, 'Look, Mummy! It's Granddad!' As he uttered the words, he turned back to the area to which he had been talking and his face fell. 'Alright, Granddad, I'll be good! Bye bye!' he said, and waved his hand in the 'bye bye' motion that small children use. 'Granddad's gone with the angels,' he told his mother, 'but he said he'll come back and see us again!'

From that day on Jamie returned to being the sunny little boy that he had been before his grandfather had died. He no longer felt that he had been abandoned by the grandfather he loved and trusted so much. He often still talked about seeing his granddad and knew he was still there for him, and that was what important to him.

What I find surprising is that all this proof is often forgotten by people as they grow older. There have been occasions when I have been speaking to ardent sceptics who have told me of their experiences seeing spirit forms as children but who now dismiss those experiences as 'nonsense' and 'imagination'. I steadfastly disagree with their thinking.

CHAPTER 16

A Friend Returns

The people from the world of spirit who care for us and watch over us whilst we blunder through our physical lives as best we can are not always family members, but people who touched upon our lives whilst they were here in their physical form and formed some type of bond with us. I have had my own experience of this.

When I arrived back in the UK after living in Australia and the breakdown of my marriage I had few friends, as the ones I had known prior to moving to the other side of the world had moved on in their own lives and consequently I seldom saw them. There was one chap, however, whom I still kept in touch with. He, unfortunately, had gone through a similar process to me in that he was now divorced and living on his own. His name was Paul. Although much of my time was immersed in my spiritual work and circle meetings, I did find time to meet up with him more or less once a week. We would go for a meal or a drink, in fact whatever took our fancy at the time. We were both free and single and getting on with our lives the best that we could. What was wonderful about Paul was the fact that he understood everything that I had gone through. He understood how difficult it was to re-establish your life as a single person once more after being in a partnership for so long. He understood my longings where my son was concerned and the fact that I missed him a great deal and was not able to be a full-time father to him.

There came a time when I was so busy that I was not able to meet up with Paul for a number of weeks and only had telephone conversations with him. During this time I did not feel happy about him. I had a nagging feeling that there was something he was not telling me. Although I was not able to spare the time for nights out, I was always there for him if he needed me and would certainly have made the time for something important. Finally I became so uneasy that I felt that the best thing I could do was to call on him and ask him if there was a problem he needed to talk about.

I telephoned Paul and told him that I was on my way around to visit him. When he opened the door I was amazed to note how much weight he had lost. I knew immediately that there was something terribly wrong. Paul invited me in and we sat down and talked. What he had been keeping from me, because he had found it difficult to admit it even to himself, was that he was terminally ill with cancer. He had not been feeling well and had visited the doctor, who had sent him for tests. These had brought the devastating news that Paul had very little time left.

I was terribly hurt that Paul had not felt able to confide in me. He explained that he had initially thought that it was going to be 'something and nothing' and did not want to burden me with something trivial. When he had received the test results, however, he was so devastated that he could not accept the news himself, let alone talk about it to anybody else.

A little more than three months after that dreadful day Paul passed peacefully on to the world of spirit. During that time we had spent many long hours talking about the world of spirit and what he could expect when the day of his passing finally arrived. I had shared with him my truths and my beliefs and he had seemed grateful and certainly more at ease during his last days.

A couple of years after Paul's passing I found myself in a situation which I was quite worried about. I was experiencing some niggling pains in my stomach. They would come and go. Sometimes they were excruciating, but other times they were barely noticeable. After a while I took myself off to my doctor for a medical examination. He said that he could find nothing particularly wrong with me and suggested a change of diet might help. This didn't put my mind at ease. I began to remember Paul and his experience. I recalled him telling me that he had also visited his doctor at the beginning of his problems and had been told that there was nothing to worry about. I decided there and then that I would go back to my doctor and insist that further investigations be carried out. I did so and an appointment was made for me to visit the hospital for tests in three weeks' time.

As I lay experiencing yet another sleepless night, an image of Paul's face suddenly drifted into my consciousness. I heard his voice in the background laughing. 'You'll never make it to those tests, Derek!' he said.

I was horrified! Was Paul telling me that I was about to join him on the spirit side of life? I had been told by spirit that I would have a long life as long as I took care of myself and exercised a personal responsibility. When I had asked Sam, all that I could get from him was that all would be well. Although this gave me comfort, I could still not help worrying.

'Oh, I know what you're thinking' Paul said, sounding more amused than ever, 'but you're wrong! You'll be in hospital well before the date of those tests – and you will be coming out again! Not like me! You'll have to wait a bit longer for your wooden overcoat!'

I didn't know whether to be happy or afraid. I just couldn't make sense of what Paul had said to me. My appointment at the hospital was in three weeks' time and I had every intention of keeping it, because I did not feel that I could continue with the problem I was having much longer. I knew that Paul had a sense of humour, but I did not appreciate his riddles.

A week later I was lying in a hospital bed recovering from surgery. I had had what at first had been thought to be appendicitis, but turned out to be something a little more serious than that. Paul was right when he told me that I would not make the date of the hospital tests.

Paul has been in visitation to me many times since that day. He always turns up when I least expect it and he always exercises his sense of humour, usually at my expense!

Julie's story is similar in that she had a friend went to the spirit world but who came back to help her.

Julie was 18 years of age. She was a lovely girl, but unfortunately was a little overweight. She had been bullied at school because of her size and Sarah, the only girl who had befriended her and stood by her, had unfortunately passed to spirit as the result of an accident. Julie had not made any friends at work because she still felt that she was not worthy of having fun. The bullying had left her with no confidence whatsoever and she was a very lonely girl. She visited my office to see whether I could tell her she had anything to look forward to in her life. I was happy to be able to tell her that she had lots of good things to look forward to, but she had to do a little work herself.

A few months later Julie wrote to me to thank me for the reading that I had conducted for her. She told me that on the day she visited me she was as close to ending it all as she could possibly get. 'You helped me though, Derek,' she said. 'You told me that I was not alone and that I should ask for help from the world of spirit and they would answer.'

Julie told me that she had gone home from my office and later that night had gone to bed and begun to dream. In her dream she had seen Sarah. She told Julie that she knew how hard a time she was having but that she was

176

there to help her. Whenever Julie thought that she was not going to make it, Sarah would be there right beside her.

When Julie woke she knew that she had not just had a dream. She felt different – more optimistic. She just knew that everything was going to be fine.

Since that day Julie has not looked back. Things have really changed for her. People began to seem more friendly towards her in her workplace, then she was asked to accompany one or two of the other girls in the office on nights out and after speaking to them about how she felt about her size, they encouraged her to lose weight. Now she has met a young man she really likes and who seems to feel the same about her. Her future is bright.

CHAPTER 17

Strangers!

There have been numerous reports of people being helped out by a stranger, only for that person to disappear immediately afterwards. But are they always strangers? My answer to that is no, they are almost never strangers, but may well be people in the spirit world who have been designated to look after us as guardians or helpers. They may be long-passed members of our family that we did not ever meet in our physical life. Whoever they are, they are there to help.

There have also been a few well-documented occasions where a number of people have experienced a similar inexplicable event in the same place. In these cases they may have been helped or guided by a spirit person who *was* a complete stranger to them. That spirit person has chosen to spend a portion of their lifetime in the spirit world guiding us mortals away from dangerous situations or events.

Linda wrote to me to tell me about her experience after being sent to a domestic violence refuge with her three small children. She says that she was miles away from home and had no family to help her. After filling in forms for benefits she was told that it would take two weeks to sort out her claim. She had no money to feed her children and was frantic with worry.

As she was standing outside the benefits office, an elderly lady seemed to appear out of nowhere and asked her what was wrong. Linda explained her dilemma to her and the lady put her hand in a bag around her waist. As she handed Linda a note she said, 'I know it's not much, but get your children some food.'

Linda thanked the lady and told her, 'You're an angel.' Then she looked down at her hand and saw a £50 pound note. She looked up and was just about to exclaim that it was far too much when she realized that the elderly lady had disappeared. There was nowhere that she could have gone in such a short time. The road was long and straight, and Linda couldn't see her anywhere.

Linda's children were amazed and kept asking their mother whether the old lady had been an angel. Linda says that she certainly saved her and her children from going hungry and gave her peace of mind until the DSS sorted out her claim. She will always be eternally grateful to the old lady who turned up out of nowhere on that day.

Was the elderly lady an angel come from the heavens to help Linda in her plight? I cannot really say! What I do know is that angels do not always come in angelic form and can sometimes be very much of the physical world. Whatever the answer to the mystery is, you can be sure that in some way the people of the spirit world had more than a small hand in the events that took place on that day.

Tim told me a story about a strange incident that happened one day as he was driving between Liverpool and Suffolk. He left Suffolk at around 6 a.m. and arrived at Watford Gap service station at about 9 a.m. to fill up with petrol. He went to pay for the petrol and on return-ing to his car found a stranger standing by the passenger door with two bags. He told Tim that he wanted a lift to Birkenhead. This stunned Tim, as there was nothing in the car to indicate that he was heading in the direction of Merseyside.

In spite of some initial reluctance, Tim agreed to give the stranger a lift and allowed him into the car. The strange man lay on the back seat and he and Tim chatted for the remainder of the journey. As they were nearing Liverpool city centre, the strange man told Tim that God had blessed his relationship and that he and his partner would go on to have a child and a happy life.

Tim says, 'As we got nearer I told him that I would drop him at Woodside, and as chance would have it, I pulled up outside the police station. He got out, shook me by the hand and I drove away. As I looked in the mirror, he disappeared from view.'

Tim has always believed that stranger to be an angel.

Shirley tells of the time that her little dog Penny ran away whilst being taken for a walk. She lives on the outskirts of a village and just didn't know where to start looking for her. She headed back home, thinking that Penny would have run there, but she hadn't. Penny means the world to Shirley and she was terribly upset at the thought of her being lost.

As Shirley was standing outside her house, wondering what to do next, a stranger pulled up in his car and told her to jump in. She unthinkingly did so. She and the stranger did not speak at all until they had reached the middle of the village. He then turned to Shirley and told her, 'You'll find her here.'

Shirley got out of the car, thanked him and he drove off in the direction from which he had come. Shirley looked around but could not see Penny. Then she noticed a little overrun pathway. Penny was there, hiding in the bushes. She was in an awful state and absolutely terrified. Shirley carried her home, washed her and cuddled her for the rest of the day.

Shirley has many questions: 'Why did this man go back in the direction he came from? Hadn't he been going somewhere? How did he know I'd lost Penny? How did he know she was hidden in the undergrowth in that particular lane?'

The ears and the eyes of the world of spirit are everywhere. I do not know whether the man in the car was an angel or a spirit person, but I very much doubt it. What I do know, though, is that whoever was at the wheel of that car was definitely being influenced by somebody in the spirit world.

Yet another story about a stranger is told by Paul. He and his mother were on a journey to visit a small community of Benedictine monks based in the Leicester area. It was a fine day, the scenery was outstanding and everything was going well. Paul and his mother talked about their beliefs and their faith in God whilst enjoying the journey.

It was not until Paul's mother started driving through the city that they started having problems finding their way. Soon they were lost and starting to panic. Suddenly the street they were travelling down seemed to clear and go very quiet. There were no people around at all except for an old man in a grey overcoat. Paul suggested to his mother that maybe they should pull over to the kerb and ask this man where to find the holy community.

Paul's mother stopped the car and Paul wound down the window and spoke to the old man. He immediately seemed aware of the fact that they were lost and gave them directions to the holy community. He told Paul that he knew where it was because he used to visit it a great deal and knew the monks there very well. Paul and his mother thanked the old man and started on the journey again, but as they turned to look back to thank him again, he had vanished into thin air and the street had begun to get busy again.

It took Paul and his mother a few minutes to arrive at the Benedictine community, where they told the monks what had happened, describing the man who had helped them and mentioning that he had said that he used to visit them regularly. One monk told Paul and his mother that no such person visited them now but a man of that description had once visited them often. Unfortunately he had died many years ago of a heart attack.

Paul comments that he felt immediate disbelief, but during the journey back home he and his mother both felt a wonderful sense of being protected by a higher power and never before had they felt so elated and happy.

Yet another incident of being helped by a stranger is related by Karen. Karen was unfortunately involved in a relationship where a lot of aggression was demonstrated towards her. One night the arguments got so bad that Karen's partner resorted to physical violence. Karen had had enough! She knew that she had to get out of the house immediately before she was seriously hurt. She was also concerned about the safety of her young son Jake.

Taking Jake with her, Karen fled the house, jumped into her car and drove off. She wanted to put as much distance between herself and her abusive partner as possible. Unfortunately, she didn't have anywhere to go, as she had moved away from the area she had grown up in to be with this man and had not had the time or opportunity to make new friends. Eventually she reached an area on the outskirts of the town where she had been living. It was quite late at night and she was at a loss as to what to do. There she was, hundreds of miles away from her family in a town that she did not know very well and responsible for a five-year-old boy. She was too embarrassed and ashamed to contact her family so late at night to tell them what had happened, as before she had left home they had warned her about the man she had become involved with and had asked her to not to move away from them and to take the relationship more slowly. Karen had ignored all their kindly advice, but now wished that she had listened.

The roads were deserted and Karen did not have enough money to even consider driving the hundreds of miles to the places she was familiar with. Apart from that, she felt both physically and mentally exhausted. She knew, however, that she would have to find somewhere to spend the night because it was far too cold to keep Jake out all night sleeping in the car.

Just as she turned a corner she saw a woman walking along the pavement. Without thinking that it was rather odd to find a woman walking on her own at such a late hour, she pulled up alongside her and wound down the passenger window.

The woman turned towards Karen's car and bent down to speak to her through the open window. Karen asked her whether she knew of any guest houses in the area that would not cost much money and would be able to put her and her son up for the night.

The woman gave her a wonderful smile. 'Of course!' she said. 'My brother has a small guest house just up this road on the right, no. 43.'

'Would you like a lift there?' asked Karen.

'No, no! I have to go somewhere else,' the woman replied. Karen thanked her and drove off in the direction she had indicated.

Reaching no. 43, Karen took Jake from the car and proceeded up the steps to the front door. She rang the bell and after a few moments the door was opened by a small dark-haired woman. Karen explained that she wanted a bed for the night and that she had been directed to this house by a lady.

'And what did this lady look like?' asked the landlady.

'She was quite slight but with fair curly hair and a wonderful smile,' Karen said. 'I thought it very strange that she would be walking alone this late at night.'

The landlady said no more but ushered Karen and Jake into the warmth of the house and showed them to a bedroom. Karen was so relieved. At least she and Jake had somewhere safe and warm to sleep. She decided that the following morning she would contact her family and ask them to transfer some money to her so that she could make the journey home to them and make a fresh start.

Morning arrived and Karen and Jake went downstairs to the dining room for breakfast. As Karen arrived in the doorway she saw a man standing by the window who bore a marked resemblance to the young woman who had helped her the night before. He turned as Karen entered the room and introduced himself as Roger. 'I believe you met my sister last night,' he said.

'Yes, I did, and I'm so grateful to her,' Karen replied. 'I would never have found your guest house without her help.'

Roger smiled. 'My sister Chris is no longer with us,' he said. 'She was murdered about six years ago now. She took up with this chap who was no good and he ended up murdering her. She didn't deserve it – she was a lovely person. It's not the first time a girl's turned up here just like you, looking for somewhere to sleep, sent here by Chris.'

Karen was astounded. She realized that the young lady who had given her directions had come from the spirit world to help her in her hour of need. Chris' spirit had recognized that Karen had found herself in a similar position to the one she herself had been in and she had been determined to help any young woman in such a situation. She had chosen this as her allotted task for the period of time that she was to remain in the world of spirit before further incarnations back into the physical world.

190

CHAPTER 18

An Angel's Warning

Life in this physical world is full of trials and tribulations. We are constantly tested and the manner in which we handle the various stumbling blocks that are placed on our pathway determines our soul growth. Some things are of course meant to be, but there are times when our guides and helpers in the world of spirit can foresee something that is about to happen that is not on our life's pathway. In these cases they attempt to warn us so that we can take evasive action. They may use other people or indeed animals to engineer a particular situation, or they may come to us in our dreams and whisper to us, warning us of some danger or harm that they have foreseen. It is up to us to listen to them.

* * *

As my grandfather Willem's time on this Earth was growing shorter, he would often sit and reminisce. There were many times in his last weeks when he used to sit up in bed talking to me in his Dutch-accented English. I may only have been young, but I found his stories fascinating and could not get enough of them.

One day he told me about a rather strange event which concerned a friend and work colleague of his. They had sailed for many years together as fishermen on trawlers sailing out of Grimsby, Hull and later Fleetwood. They used to disappear off to sea for four days, heading for the fishing points they had trawled many times before.

On one particular trip my grandfather's friend, Hendrix, was particularly quiet. At the end of the first day's work my grandfather asked him what was the matter, as he was usually a very jovial and happy man, but Hendrix would not be drawn. He told my grandfather that he did not want to talk about what was bothering him. Not wishing to upset his friend, my grandfather respected his wish and they both got on with their work, though Granddad was concerned to see the change in his friend.

That night they went to bed. There were no luxury cabins on the trawlers in my grandfather's days as a fisherman, merely shared cabins with barely enough space to turn around in. Consequently any belongings had to be safely and neatly stowed. Anything left lying around would not only be a danger whilst the ship bobbed around on the rough seas but would also take up valuable space in the very cramped conditions. My grandfather and Hendrix lay down on their separate bunks and fell asleep.

Granddad told me that he then began to have the most sensational dream. He dreamed of a wonderful place – 'a heaven', he called it. It was full of bright light, beautiful peace and happiness. There were people walking around and he could tell they were very happy. Nobody was old or infirm, but there were children running around and laughing.

'And then a young man separated himself from the crowd, Derek,' said Granddad. 'He walked over to me and said, "You must help him. You are the only person who can help!" "Help who?" I asked.'

Granddad was bemused. He did not understand why he should need to help anybody because as far as he knew, nobody needed help.

Then Granddad gradually became aware of a noise in the cabin. As he slowly woke he could hear something banging loudly. He leaned across to a small locker and lit the lamp which was fixed to the top of it. By the light of the lamp he was amazed to see that everything that had been so neatly stowed away when he and Hendrix had retired to bed was now lying on the tiny floor space of the cabin. A pair of heavy boots was banging against the door as they slid around with the movement of the trawler. And Hendrix was no longer in his bunk.

In a flash Granddad knew that there was something terribly wrong. He recalled the words of the young man in his dream. Normally, had he woken up and noted that one of the crew was absent from their bunk he would have thought nothing of it, but this time he knew that he had to get up and go to find Hendrix.

Granddad scrambled into his clothes and rushed up the stairs and out onto the cold and windy deck. He looked around him but could see nobody. He raced to the other end of the trawler and was just in time to see Hendrix beginning to climb over the safety rail.

'*Hendrix!*' he screamed as he raced the few yards between his friend and himself. 'Don't! Whatever it is, we can sort it out! Nothing's worth this!'

To Granddad's great relief Hendrix seemed to slump when he heard those words and he managed to grab hold of him and drag him off the safety rail. If he had arrived on deck only a moment or two later, it would have been too late – Hendrix would have thrown himself overboard and would have been lost to the waves forever.

Granddad half-carried/half-dragged Hendrix to the safety of the galley, where they sat down.

'Now Hendrix! You and I have known each other for so long. Can you not tell your old friend what is bothering you?' Granddad said.

Hendrix broke down and began to tell Granddad that his wife had walked off and left him. When he had returned from his last trip he had found an empty home. His wife had taken everything. He just did not know what to do.

I do not know what advice my grandfather gave Hendrix, but what I do know is that the two men remained friends for many a long year. In fact it had only been a year or two earlier that my grandfather had sadly received the news of Hendrix's passing.

'And the moral of my story, Derek, is to listen to the angels,' said Granddad. 'I know that night when Hendrix tried to throw himself overboard I was visited by an angel in my dreams. If it had not been for that dream I would not have bothered going to find Hendrix. I'm sure that it was the same angel who wakened me by messing up our belongings, causing the boots to knock against the door.'

Louise was expecting a baby. Everything had been going well and no problems were envisaged with the birth. One night she was sitting on the floor watching television when her mother's dog came over and sat down in front of her. Without warning he lunged forward and nipped her face, drawing blood. He then walked away and sat in his basket.

Everybody was terribly shocked, as the dog usually adored Louise and was a very gentle and kind creature. Louise says that she should have shouted at him and been very angry, but for some reason she wasn't and she prevented her husband from telling him off as well.

Because she was expecting a baby Louise thought it best to telephone the hospital to tell them what had happened and arrange to have the bite checked. They requested that she call in the following morning.

When morning arrived Louise felt very sick and groggy, but because she knew she had to visit the hospital she got up out of bed. At the hospital, the bite was checked and at the same time, as a precautionary measure, the medical staff decided to conduct tests using a monitor. This displayed that Louise was in fact in labour and due to give birth in spite of the fact that she was only 26 weeks pregnant.

After enormous problems and a heroic effort by the hospital team, Louise's baby was born. Unfortunately she was a very sick child, as she was so under-developed, and it was not expected that she would survive. For a time everything looked terribly grim. A week later the baby began to improve slightly, but Louise and her husband were told that there was a chance that their daughter would be brain-damaged. She was in hospital for some 13 weeks, but eventually she pulled through. No one could explain her survival, as she had been so terribly ill. She is now six years old and Louise describes her as 'fantastic and very clued up'.

The people in the world of spirit work in mysterious ways. If the pet dog had not been influenced to uncharacteristically nip Louise, causing her to go to hospital when she did and put herself in the right place at the right time, no doubt her baby would not have survived. As Louise says, 'Tell me an angel is not looking after her! I believe she is constantly being looked after and was meant to be!'

Out of the blue one evening Catherine became increasingly aware that someone close to her was at risk. She is certain that somebody put this idea into her head. She knew for certain that it was not herself or her child who would be at risk, but she felt that she would be affected by something that was going to happen to her partner.

By nine o'clock in the evening Catherine had become so agitated that her partner had begun to notice her change of mood. The feeling of panic deepened and her partner said that she was beginning to make him feel very nervous too. They both had trouble sleeping that night. The following morning, 7 July 2005, they were both awoken by an emergency call from her partner's work calling him to duty in central London to cover the London bombings. As he left the house, they both cried. Thankfully Catherine's partner was not directly involved in any of the bombings and returned home safely after a harrowing day.

To this day Catherine says that neither of them can explain why she felt that he was in impending danger. My answer to that is that not all danger is physical – it can sometimes be mental. Some people are more sensitive than others and what will affect one person radically may not affect another person quite so badly. Catherine was being warned by somebody in the spirit world that something awful was about to take place and that in some way her partner would be involved.

A very important warning was received by Pete. Unfortunately he had been very heavily involved in solvent abuse from a young age. His habit had continued to the point where he began hearing voices, all of which he put down to the mind-altering substances he was taking – all, that is, but one! This particular voice stood out in

Pete's mind. He said that it was really the only one he could clearly remember hearing, as the rest were just overlapping nonsensical babble.

This voice would talk to Pete about what would happen if he kept abusing solvents. Gradually he began to take notice of what was being said to him and the voice eventually persuaded him to stop his habit before it killed him.

'Although I didn't see any angels or apparitions, I was definitely warned by a spirit,' Pete states.

Pete can be assured that he was contacted directly by a loved one in the world of spirit. That person could not bear to see him wasting his life in the way that he was. They wanted him to achieve all that he could in this physical lifetime and knew that if he continued on the pathway that he was then walking, this would not be possible.

CHAPTER 19

Wings of an Angel

All the people I have spoken to who have experienced true angelic visitation have mentioned that the first awareness they had that something unusual was about to happen was a rustling sound. They have likened it to the noise that the feathers of a large bird make when it spreads and flaps its wings before settling them back down to the side of its body. I have to agree with them. As previously mentioned, I have had two experiences where an angelic force has come to me, and on both occasions my first awareness was a dry rustling noise. This was followed almost immediately by the most beautiful emotions and peace.

In contrast I have of course experienced spirit visitation on thousands of occasions. When a spirit person makes their presence felt or allows a person to see them there is little or no noise. Any noise that can be heard is always attributable to the rustling of clothing or to the fact that the spirit person has moved an item of furniture or an ornament, etc.

Elsie knew that an angel had visited her. She had woken in the early hours of the morning with a start and had heard a very strange rustling noise. Then suddenly at the end of her bed, not moving but just standing staring at her, there had appeared a very tall being surrounded by a brilliant white light.

'I could've sworn this figure had wings, Derek. I could see each individual feather and it looked like a bird's wing,' Elsie told me, 'and it was dressed in what looked like a long flowing robe – just like you see in the pictures! I couldn't tell whether it was a man or a woman, but I knew that whatever or whoever it was, it was definitely an angel.'

Elsie went on to tell me that prior to seeing the angel she had been feeling rather unwell and been really quite concerned over her health. After the visit, though, she knew that all would be well – and it was.

I used to see Elsie now and again in Liverpool city centre with her friend Ada, and she would always remind me of her first angelic visitation. 'I've seen it since, you know, Derek,' she told me on one occasion. 'Every time

I'm feeling unwell my angel friend comes and stands at the bottom of my bed and I know that I'll be feeling better the following day.'

Two or three years passed and I no longer had my office in Liverpool and therefore did not visit the city centre much at all. One day, however, I had to travel to the city and took the opportunity to take a walk around the streets just as I had in the old days. I was not surprised to see all the old familiar faces on the stalls and in the shops, but I was certainly surprised to see Ada trotting along on her own. She and Elsie always went out together.

I shouted, 'Ada!' and she turned round. 'Where's Elsie?' I asked her.

Ada looked terribly sad as she told me that Elsie had passed away not long after I had left my office in Victoria Street. 'Right to the end she kept talking about her angel,' she told me. 'The only difference was, it didn't stand at the bottom of the bed like it used to – it'd stand right next to her bed. She'd tell me that as soon as she heard that rustling noise, she knew her angel was on its way!'

I was saddened to think that I would not be bumping into Elsie any more. She was such a character and a chat with her was like a tonic. I was happy to know that her angel had been alongside her right to the end.

* * *

Sheila was on holiday in Cyprus with her husband. She was sound asleep when she was suddenly woken by what she initially thought was birds in the bedroom. There was the furious sound of flapping wings above her head and when she raised her head from the pillow there was a 'whoosh' and she saw 'a trail of something strange' disappear. Sheila says that she cannot say that she saw an angel, but she instinctively knew that what she had experienced was indeed an angel.

The morning after Sheila's experience her mother was due to go to hospital for a minor test to assess a problem she had been having. Sheila's aunt was accompanying her and they expected to be at the hospital for only a day.

At 2 o'clock in the afternoon Sheila telephoned the hospital for news of her mother's progress and was shocked to be told that her mum had 'arrested' immediately after the test. However, the staff had managed to resuscitate her and she was now in a high-dependency ward. Sheila was advised to fly home, as the doctors did not think her mother would make it through the following night.

Thankfully Sheila's mother survived, though she had to face major surgery for the lung cancer that had been discovered during the test.

Sheila tells me that in hindsight she truly believes that angels were warning her of impending doom that night in Cyprus, but that they were also telling her that it would be alright. 'Nobody will ever change my feelings about this,' she states.

Wanda also told me about being woken up by the sound of wings beating loudly and a 'whooshing' noise. This took place at a time when she was feeling quite down about her life. When she was woken by the strange noise, she says she felt a warm wind rush over her. Then she felt a huge soft wing brush across her. It left her feeling warm and happy.

Wanda wonders whether it was an angel who had come to comfort her as she had just gone through five years of struggle.

CHAPTER 20

Angelic Animals

I am always amazed by the number of people who find it difficult to accept that animals are as much a spark of the infinite as we are. When their life in the physical world comes to an end, they pass over to the world of spirit in exactly the same way that we do. They have spirit souls just as we do so, why on Earth shouldn't they pass on to the world of spirit? Why shouldn't they return to the place from whence they came, just as we do?

Over the years I have been practising mediumship I have lost count of the number of animals from the spirit world who have returned during the course of a sitting to let their former owners know that they are happy, healthy and being cared for. They cannot of course converse with me any more than they could when they were here in their physical form, but their demeanour and aura convey to me that their well-being is being taken care of. The joy that they demonstrate when they manifest at the feet of a beloved human companion is immeasurable.

Animals will be in visitation to the homes they left behind in exactly the same way and for the same reasons as spirit people will return to their homes and families. They are drawn by the bond of love – love which continues beyond physical death.

Animals may not have the intellect of humans, but they are just as aware of life's ups and downs. My own animals instinctively know if I am sad. They come close to me and rest their heads on my hands. Their looks convey the message that they know I am down or have a problem and they are there for me. If I am happy, they are exuberant and playful. If I am tired, they lie down to sleep with me. If I am working at home, they lie by my side and wait patiently for the time when work ceases and a long walk across the fields is in the offing. No words are necessary. Love goes beyond words. Why should this change when our beloved animals pass over to the world of spirit? Let me tell you that it most definitely does not!

As I have explained in earlier chapters, although our lives are mapped out for us before we even incarnate once more into the physical world, various tests are placed along the way. Some are meant for us, but others are not. We can find ourselves in the wrong place at the wrong time and it is then that the people from the world of spirit are allowed to step in and alter the course of events. It sometimes happens that a beloved animal is encouraged to manifest in order to draw our attention and divert us from something that is not meant for us.

Although I cannot claim that an animal in spirit has saved my life or the life of any person close to me by warning of impending danger, I can tell you about an animal in spirit stepping forward and saving the life of another animal.

At the time Gwen and I had four cats, Mork, Mindy, Toby and Jasper. We had previously had a fifth cat, Tiddles, who had passed on to the spirit world some 12 months earlier. Down towards the bottom of our garden there was a large fishpond which was very deep and had crazy paving surrounding it. Its walls were straight and sheer in order to discourage marauding herons from stopping by to breakfast on the ornamental fish.

I was looking out of the kitchen window one day when I noticed a cat pacing up and down the side of the pond. It was a most unusual thing for a cat to do and as I looked harder I realized that the cat I was seeing was in fact

Tiddles. I shouted to Gwen to come and look. I know that Gwen desperately misses the pets that we have lost to the spirit world and would love to see them again for herself.

Gwen came rushing into the kitchen, but unfortunately could see nothing. Tiddles meanwhile continued to pace backwards and forwards by the fishpond. 'What an odd thing for him to be doing,' Gwen commented. 'I'm going out to see what's going on.'

She walked down the garden. As she did so Tiddles' spirit form disappeared from my view. Gwen approached the pond and as she did so she suddenly rushed forward then turned and waved agitatedly and yelled to me to get to the pond as quickly as I could.

By the time I reached it Gwen was lying flat on her front trying to grab something. I realized that it was Mork, our ginger and white cat, who had obviously fallen into the pond and was frantically attempting to get out. Because the sides of the pond were so straight he could not get a foothold in order to haul himself up and was just frantically paddling away to keep his head above the surface of the water. He was weakening, however, and if we had arrived only a few moments later, he would have drowned.

Tiddles had returned to save his old friend from a watery grave. He had drawn my attention to him and acted in such a way as to cause Gwen to question what was going on.

Mork, meanwhile, was a very relieved cat. He was brought into the house to have his coat cleaned and to be dried off. He spent the rest of the day sleeping. The fishpond was immediately covered with a wire cage in order to prevent any further accidents.

Mary had a small dog named Toby. He was of no particular breed, being what is known in Liverpool as a 'Heinz 57'. This did not matter to Mary. She loved Toby almost more than anything else in the world. He was her constant companion and kept her company throughout the long evenings when nobody else was around.

When Toby was about 15 years of age he passed suddenly to the world of spirit. Mary was devastated. She did not know how she was going to live without her little dog.

One day some weeks after Toby's departure to the spirit world Mary was walking to the shops near her home when she suddenly spied Toby. She was certain that it was him because this dog had exactly the same markings and exactly the same jaunty walk and tilt of the head. There was something strange, though. He did not seem as 'solid' as he had been, more ethereal. Mary realized that she was seeing the spirit form of her beloved Toby. She was determined to try to get closer to him.

As she walked towards Toby, he ducked and darted away down a small pathway which led along the side of a house. Mary followed. It was a dead end. Just as she reached the end she heard an enormous crashing sound. She turned around hurriedly and to her horror saw an overturned wagon that had obviously gone out of control and crashed. It was now on its side, lying sprawled across the road and pavement. It had come to rest hard up against the front of the house along which the pathway ran. Mary realized that if Toby had not diverted her down the path she would have been crushed by the vehicle.

Mary hurried back towards the scene of the accident. People had gathered around waiting for the police to come and for an ambulance to arrive to tend to the lorry driver who, although very dazed, did not appear to be too badly hurt.

'You're lucky,' a woman in the crowd commented to Mary. 'I saw you walking along the pavement just a second before the wagon skidded into the wall and I was convinced you were trapped underneath it. It was only when I saw you just now that I realized you were alright!'

Mary is convinced that Toby saved her life, that he came back in his spirit form to lead her a merry dance so that she would not be in the pathway of the vehicle. I am firmly in agreement with her.

Happily, Mary now has a new puppy. She has called him Simon. Simon will never replace Toby, but he is providing Mary with the love and companionship she once enjoyed with her beloved old friend.

Bobby told me about his Belgian Shepherd dog Arnie. Arnie unfortunately passed to the world of spirit a year ago. Bobby explained that it was a terrible time for him and his family, as they all adored Arnie, and they have only just started to get over their grief. However, Arnie comes back to visit those he loved so much. He makes himself known to Bobby by lying on the end of his bed some nights, just as he did before his passing to spirit.

A couple of months after Arnie's passing Bobby and his family were travelling in their car when the brakes suddenly cut out. Bobby's father was forced to pull over to the side of the road. Everybody alighted from the car. Bobby's father went to open the bonnet, but seconds before he was able to do so the steering wheel section caught fire and the whole car was engulfed in flames.

The cause of the fire was a tube coming loose, but there was no explanation for the brakes cutting out as they did. Bobby attributes his family's narrow escape from disaster to Arnie, who was watching over them from the spirit world and keeping them safe.

A golden retriever passes in and out of the life of Jenny and her family. It always appears when something troublesome has occurred, and when they see it, they know everything is going to be alright. It is strange that they have never owned such a dog themselves and can only assume that it is a dog which lived in the house that is now their home and which returns in visitation when it feels that the family is in need of a friendly face.

Fiona's cat Benji was with her for almost 16 years. She considered him the love of her life and always felt that when it was time for him to pass to the world of spirit her own life would end too. Of course, this was not the case and although she missed her pet dreadfully, Fiona was very soon delighted to be aware that Benji had not left at all but was in constant visitation in spirit form. He would curl up on her bed just as he had during his physical life and she would often hear him purring as he sat in his favourite place on a sunny window ledge.

Fiona had made arrangements to attend a motor rally, but as the day drew nearer she began to feel that she would prefer not to go. However, she was taking another two people with her in her car and she felt that she could not let them down. The night before the event she felt Benji jump onto her bed, but instead of curling up and settling down as he normally did, she had the distinct impression that he was scrabbling around and scratching frantically at the covers as if he was trying to pass on some sort of urgent message. She just knew that he did not want her to attend the rally the following day.

The following morning Fiona felt even more uneasy about attending the event, but didn't feel that she could avoid it because of the two people who were relying upon her for transport. With some trepidation she climbed into her car and drove off, much disturbed by the events that had taken place the night before.

When Fiona and her two friends arrived at the rally, however, everything seemed to go well. Gradually Fiona began to relax and enjoy herself and wondered why she had felt so nervous and insecure over attending.

The day had started off hot and dry, but as the afternoon wore on clouds began to gather and during one of the races it began to absolutely pour down with rain. Fiona was sheltering under a marquee that was located some way back from the track and just past a rather hazardous corner. As the cars careered around this corner, one of them skidded, bounced off and through the bales of straw edging the racetrack and carried on, completely out of control, in the direction of the marquee. Fortunately, it ground to a halt before it collided with the marquee, but amid the screaming and rushing to get away from the route of the vehicle, Fiona tripped and twisted her foot badly. She was stretchered to the first aid post and from there was taken by ambulance to the local hospital, where an X-ray revealed that she had broken two small bones in her foot.

Fiona is grateful that she suffered minimal injury and that nobody else was hurt during the unfortunate incident, and she realized immediately that her beloved Benji had been warning her that she should not attend the rally.

'In future,' she told me, 'I won't be ignoring Benji! He's definitely my guardian angel!'

CHAPTER 21

A Premonition

I am sure that everybody can recall a time when they have 'just known' that something was about to happen. Maybe they have thought about a person they have not seen for quite a while and then have suddenly bumped into that person or received a telephone call from them. Sometimes people have a 'gut' feeling that they should not do something or go somewhere because they know that if they do, things will not work out for them. I would say that they are being warned to take care by their guides and helpers in the world of spirit.

Paul's premonition came to him in a dream. He describes it as probably the most vivid dream he has ever had in his life. He writes:

'I have been able to work out the exact date of my dream. This dream has had the greatest impact on me and has caused me to reassess myself, the physical world we live in and really practically everything we know to be real. It was on the night of Wednesday 14 January 1998 that I dreamed in real dream format, in vivid detail, my own death. I was going to be killed in a head-on collision with a truck on the mountainous section of the Mount Lindsay highway. It was going to happen at a specific corner and involve a very large semi-trailer which was green and brown in colour. The location was past Palen Creek at the corner of the small cutting just below Mount Lindsay itself.'

Paul tells me that in his dream, after the impact, he knew that he had suffered a fatal wound to his head and that he had died almost instantly. He can remember feeling confused and worried about his family after he had left his physical body but what he describes as 'an entity' was with him and told him not to worry and that he was being taken somewhere. He was shown to what he describes as a 'huge white marble place' and then taken to a group of people. He was amazed to recognize an uncle who had recently passed on to the spirit world, an aunt and his grandmother, and there were several other people there as well whom he did not recognize. He started talking to his uncle, who gestured with his finger to his lips, 'Shhhh!' It was not until some time later that Paul realized that the uncle he had attempted to speak to had been profoundly deaf in life and yet in the dream he had heard Paul's voice. Upon looking through some family photographs at a later date, Paul also discovered that the people he had not recognized in his dream were in fact members of his family whom he had never met.

Paul knew that in several weeks he would be going on holiday to the Clarence River wilderness lodge and would be driving along the very road where he had had the accident in his dream. He was frantic, as he believed that he only had two weeks to live. For the first couple of days after the dream he was petrified. He could not discuss it with his wife, as he believed she would think he was crazy. As the days went by, he began to appreciate the world he lived in – colours were brighter, smells were more intense – and he began experiencing a feeling of serenity, but he knew that he did not want to die. Eventually, as 24 January drew closer, he decided to discuss his dream with his wife, regardless of what she might think. Her response was that it was only a dream and that they should look forward to their holiday.

On the morning of 24 January Paul and his wife headed off on holiday. He still had huge reservations about travelling along the Mount Lindsay highway, as it was a narrow and winding road that required intense concentration. He decided that he would drive very slowly, as he believed that nothing could happen if he drove at that pace.

As Paul approached the area of the highway that he had seen in his dream, there was an old grey-haired driver in front of him. He thought to himself that whilst there was a driver in front it would be impossible for him to be involved in a head-on collision, so he stayed patiently behind, but then, to his consternation, just as he was approaching the dreaded section of the road, the elderly driver pulled over and indicated to Paul to pass him.

Paul overtook him, but continued to drive slowly and cautiously. Then, as he was driving down a hill, he saw in the distance the very truck he had seen in his dream. It was exact in every detail. Paul realized that the only way he could avert the inevitable was to drive as slowly as he possibly could.

It was just as well that he did! As he approached the corner that he dreaded so much, the huge green and brown truck came around it, cutting the corner so badly that its back wheels cut through the gutter on the side of the road where Paul would have been driving had he not had the foresight to drive so slowly. If he had been there five seconds earlier his car would have been destroyed and neither he nor his wife would have survived!

Paul's 'dream' is a marvellous example of spirit people forewarning a person of a dangerous situation which could prove fatal but in fact is not meant for them. Our loved ones often come to us in our dreams in an attempt to persuade us to make the correct decisions. Thank goodness Paul took notice of his dream. If he had just dismissed it out of hand, his story would have ended very, very differently.

David's mother had a dream on Christmas Eve. In it she saw her family travelling along a motorway in their car when there was a tyre blowout. The car spun across all three lanes of traffic before eventually coming to rest against the barrier at the edge of the hard shoulder.

Two days later, the family was in the car on the way to visit relatives. David's father was driving. Suddenly there was a bang and the car spun out of control. David's mother grabbed hold of David and pulled him towards his sister, who was also sitting on the rear seat of the car. 'I just knew that David's side of the car would be the point of impact,' she later told people. And it was. When the vehicle eventually came to rest against the metal fence at the side of the road, the part of the car where David had been sitting was crushed. If he had still been in his seat, he would have been badly hurt. His mother's warning from the spirit world saved him from harm.

Celia had been coming along to my office in Liverpool for a number of years. She was an air hostess with one of the companies providing long-haul flights. She loved her job and was grateful to be able to see the world. She used to visit me once a year, 'just for a top up', as she would say with a laugh.

One year when Celia arrived for her annual 'top up' she was bursting to tell me about a dream that she had had and the events that had taken place afterwards.

Celia dreamed that she was at work during a crowded flight to Australia. She remembers feeling nervous and edgy during her dream, as though something was about to happen but she was not quite sure what. Suddenly, as she looked out of the window of the aeroplane, she saw sheets of flame passing by. An alarm sounded and she and the rest of the cabin crew started rushing around trying to calm the passengers. Celia told me that in the dream she was absolutely terrified. She woke up suddenly, but the feeling of dread remained with her. She just did not want to go to work that day, as she was scheduled to fly to Australia.

Contrary to Celia's expectations, however, the flight out to the Antipodes was smooth and unremarkable. The stops were made as scheduled and she began to scold herself for being so silly as to take notice of a dream. She relaxed in Sydney for a couple of days before undertaking the return flight to the UK, when again she would be working as a flight attendant.

Celia had more or less forgotten all about her dream by this time, but as she busied herself in the galley just a few moments before take-off, the details all came flooding back to her. As the plane taxied forward, a sudden shout was heard from one of the passengers: 'Fire! The plane's on fire!'

Celia looked out of one of the windows and saw flames shooting up from somewhere around the starboard wing. She and the rest of the flight staff swung into their emergency routine as the pilot radioed for assistance. As the red tenders of the fire department raced across the tarmac towards the aeroplane, Celia and the rest of the staff were calming down the passengers and preparing for their disembarkation.

'D'you know, Derek,' she said, 'that terrifying time was almost a carbon copy of my dream! The only thing that

231

was different was that in my dream the plane was in the air, whilst the fire actually happened whilst the plane was still on the ground!'

I nodded. I could hear Celia's mother in the world of spirit tut-tutting in the background. 'Well, I couldn't let anything happen to our Celia,' she said. 'It wasn't time for her to come over here. I tried to warn her to stay away from the Australian flight, but she wouldn't listen to me!'

Who knows what would have happened if that flight had taken place without Celia on board? Would the fire have broken out during the flight? Would the plane have been able to limp to another airport and land safely? We will never know! I doubt very much that a fatal accident would have taken place, however, as if that had been the case and people had been meant to go over to the spirit world, Celia's mother would not have been able to intervene in order to save her daughter. What is certain is that Celia had a premonition about the events that were about to take place.

Celia continued to enjoy her job as a flight attendant for many more years until she finally met and married the young man of her dreams and settled down to family life with their two children. I doubt very much, though, that she will ever forget the night that she dreamed about a flaming aeroplane!

* * *

A Premonition

Premonitions do not always warn of danger to the recipient. People can also be warned that something untoward is about to happen.

A lady named Julie visited me at my office and prior to her reading told me about two incidents that had taken place.

Julie told me that as she parked her car in a multi-storey car park one day, she just felt that she should not leave it in that spot and that if she did it would not be there upon her return. Sure enough, when she returned to retrieve her vehicle, it had disappeared! After fruitlessly searching through every level of the car park, she reported the loss to the police. The car was recovered some days later, totally wrecked.

A similar incident occurred when Julie was travelling abroad with her husband. They had hired a car to explore the area in which they were staying and as her husband parked it up in a side street, Julie had the distinct feeling that they should move it to another place. In spite of knowing about her previous premonition, however, her husband decided that it would be safe where it was. When they returned to it, they discovered that it had sustained a considerable amount of damage, together with two others, when a large vehicle had attempted to traverse the narrow street and had struck the row of parked cars.

* * *

Robert wrote to tell me that until around two years ago he would have considered himself something of a sceptic concerning spirits, angels, and so on, but over the past couple of years he had become more interested in guardian angels, past lives and the world beyond. It was because of this interest that he had been able to understand some bizarre events.

In Robert's own words:

'In 1992 I was involved in a bad crash on my way home from work one night. The passenger in the other vehicle died from her injuries. I was 20 years old at the time and the following court case pushed me into terrible depression. I was later told by a doctor who attended the scene that I should not have walked away from the accident.

'For two years I battled with weight, depression and drink, but through all the depths of despair I felt there was always a guiding hand. I soon met some new friends who helped me get my life back together. Were these chance meetings or was I again being guided into this situation?

A Premonition

'It was around mid-1997 that I started to have premonitions of car accidents. There would be a dream of a car hitting the back of another – not violently, though – and this dream would play over and over in my head throughout my working hours.

'The first time I experienced this it lasted two days. I thought that it was just a throwback to my first accident, then on the second day I was on my way home from work and was involved in an accident at a set of traffic lights. No one was hurt and after that the scene that had been playing in my head stopped.

'I had this happen on a further two occasions, but these times the drivers involved were other members of my family. It was strange because I would have the same dream as before, then when I was awake this again would play over but then just stop. I would later find out that the time it stopped was the time that they had their accidents. Fortunately, no one was injured.

'A couple of years ago I became interested in the paranormal and wanted to understand it a bit more. A couple of my friends were also interested. One of *these friends knew that she had someone who watched over her. She also used to do tarot card readings. One night last year we all got together and my tarot cards were read. I became very sceptical about the whole paranormal thing and started to think that it was all parlour games and tricks, but when I got home I had a bizarre dream. In it I saw a footbridge with people on it which then became fractured. The next image I saw was a passenger jetliner with its left-wing engine on fire. I woke up. It was about 5 a.m. on a Sunday morning and I wrote down what I had seen and then went back into a fitful sleep. I then had a dream of a woman standing there. She had a reassuring look on her face.*

'I got up around 10 a.m. and switched on the television. I could not believe my eyes. On the Sky News channel was the breaking headline "Airport Accident". I froze to the spot. A suspended walkway at a French airport had collapsed! As I continued watching the news they then showed the Concorde that had crashed at the same airport with the same engine and wing on fire as I had seen!

A Premonition

*'I believe the woman I saw was an angel who was
maybe reaffirming that there was a way for spirits
and angels to communicate and telling me not to close
up.'*

I would say to everybody, always listen to your inner voice.
If you have a feeling that something is not quite right, then
heed it – it may be a warning from the world beyond that
everything is not as it should be.

CHAPTER 22

Reassurance

There are times in all our lives when we experience trauma. It is at these times that our family in the world of spirit, our guides and our guardians draw ever closer. Whether that trauma is part of our ultimate destiny or something that has been placed on our pathway for us to deal with in the best way that we can, we all appreciate a little support.

Even when things are running smoothly, there are also times when we need that extra little bit of encouragement in life. We all enjoy a pat on the shoulder or a word of encouragement, even though the going may not be so tough. In short, we always like a little bit of reassurance that we are doing well and making a good job of the difficult task of conducting our lives in the physical world.

Dawn was definitely one such person. Although she had a happy home life, a job and no particular cares, she still felt that she was not doing quite enough, that there was something she should be doing but was not. She could never put her finger on the cause of her concerns, but it did get to a point where she began worrying unnecessarily about her life in general. It might have been her intuition warning her that something was about to happen, but that was not the case – nothing untoward did happen. Dawn's life carried on as normal, with no upheavals and no ripples affecting the calm of her existence.

Nevertheless Dawn reached a point where she was beginning to find it difficult to fall asleep. One night she was lying in bed worrying about nothing as usual. Her bedroom was in total darkness due to heavy curtains, but she suddenly became aware of a light at the end of her bed. It started off as a glow but then grew and became brighter and more intense. Dawn watched in amazement as it grew both wider and taller. When it reached the point where it was almost as high as the ceiling, it narrowed to a shape resembling a person, though it was much taller than any person would be. Dawn describes the light as 'rippling and running like water overflowing from a basin – like a huge cascade'. She did not see any features or even the true shape of a person, but she knew that it was her guardian angel. She did not feel scared but calm and comfortable and at peace. She felt as though this brilliant light had washed over her and taken her cares away.

Then Dawn heard a voice. It was not a voice she recognized and she could not distinguish whether it was a man's or a woman's voice. She is not even sure whether she heard it aurally at all or whether the words were in her head. They were: 'Stop worrying. Everything is as it should be.'

As the light diminished and faded, Dawn fell asleep. She slept the whole night through without wakening and in the morning she felt refreshed and optimistic. From that day onward she was able to get on with her life without the feelings of agitation and depression that she had been experiencing for so long. She knows that she was visited by her guardian angel.

Jane tells of an instance when her mother was standing at her father's graveside. She was grieving deeply for her husband and finding it hard to go on. Then she heard a man say, 'It will be OK, you know.'

When she looked up there was a kind-faced man dressed all in white standing beside her. As she looked at him she felt a sudden sense of peace and replied to him, 'I know it will, thank you.'

She turned to look briefly at her husband's grave once more and when she turned back towards the man, he had gone.

Jane is convinced that the person was an angel who came to bring reassurance to her mother and help her through her grief.

Stacey remembers a time when her small daughter was quite ill. She was very worried about her and could not sleep. In the early hours of the morning she went to her room to check on her. As she stepped inside the room she saw a bright white light at the foot of her daughter's bed. In the midst of the white light stood a young man. He slowly lifted his arms up from his side and as he did so the bright light travelled up the bed until the bed and the little girl were within it. Stacey felt at peace and reassured that everything would be alright from then on. And it was!

Sue tells me that after her father died she was so upset she used to drink herself into oblivion every night. One Saturday evening her grandson Liam came to stay. When he had gone to bed Sue opened the whiskey bottle and after a few drinks fell asleep on the sofa. She was woken by Liam screaming. She rushed into his room to find him curled up at one end of the bed and pointing to the other end. 'Get that fairy away from me!' he was screaming. Sue tried to tell him that there was nothing there, but he was inconsolable and shaking and kept crying about the 'fairy'. In the end Sue took him downstairs and settled him down on the couch with her.

The following morning Sue took Liam to church with her. Once inside the church Liam picked up a book and settled down to read it. He suddenly shouted, 'That's that fairy that scared me, Nana!'

Sue and her daughter looked at the picture and saw that it was of angels. Sue says that the hairs stood up on the back of her neck as she realized that Liam had seen an angel. Her daughter felt frightened. Sue asked Liam if the angel had said anything. He replied, 'Gangan Jack alright now!'

After that day Sue has never needed whiskey to get to sleep. She has had the confirmation that her dad is 'alright'!

When Jack's father was rushed to hospital with complete heart failure, he was not expected to survive. As Jack stood with his mother outside the Accident & Emergency room late that night, they were convinced that they would never see him alive again. Jack sat down on a chair and put his head in his hands. Suddenly he heard a rather chirpy man's voice telling him, 'He'll be alright, you know! It's not his time yet!'

Jack was astounded. He looked about him to see if anybody was close by, but nobody was there. His mother had wandered over to the other side of the room and was staring worriedly out of the window into the darkness. She was the only other person around, as the medical team was quite a way down the hospital corridor attempting to resuscitate Jack's father. Jack was even more astounded when he realized that the voice that he had heard was that of his Uncle Bill, his father's brother, who had passed to the spirit world some years earlier. Jack always remembered him for his jovial personality and sense of fun.

Jack told his mother what had happened. She looked at him rather doubtfully and said that it must have been his imagination playing games with him.

At that moment the doctor came striding towards them. 'Your husband should not be alive!' he told Jack's mother. 'But he is, and what's more, his condition is stable and we expect that without complications he will recover!'

Jacks told me that the relief that he and his mother felt at that moment cannot be described.

On the following day, when he and his mother were at home, he spoke once more to her about the words he had heard at the hospital.

'Perhaps it wasn't your imagination after all, son,' she said. 'Perhaps Bill was there and wanted us to know that we shouldn't have worried quite so much.'

CHAPTER 23

One Good Deed …

I am a great believer in karma. If you do something to somebody that is hurtful or harmful, then you can be sure that at some point that hurt or harm will be returned to you. If, on the other hand, you do something that will benefit another person or persons, then you know that you will have blessings aplenty and will receive only goodness in return. I have seen the laws of 'cause and effect' proved time and time again during my lifetime.

There have been occasions in my own life when people have been less than kind to me or have caused me unnecessary and undeserved heartache. What do I do with these people? I bless them and send them on their way, because

I know that at some point in time they will have to suffer the consequences of their actions. They will receive heartache and hurt in equal measure to that which they unjustifiably dished out to me.

But, as already mentioned, by the same token a person who is kind and charitable towards another can expect kindness in return. Karmic debts and karmic credits are always repaid.

I recall a young man in his early thirties. He was a very spiritual man and his name was Frank. He had been married and had a young son, but unfortunately the marriage had not been successful. Nobody was to blame, it had just not worked out. He had done what he considered to be the 'decent thing' and had left his wife and son with everything and had walked away with merely a suitcase containing a few clothes.

Frank had a job as a security guard at a well-known store. Eventually he met a young lady of whom he became very fond, but yet again the relationship faltered after a while because the young lady in question developed a roving eye. Frank was a great believer in fidelity and could not cope with the idea that he had been let down. He was dreadfully upset at what had happened, but resolved that in future he would not become too involved with a person too quickly.

A year or so passed. Frank met another young lady, but he had not learned his lesson. In fact this time he compounded his error because after a few short months he found himself a married man once more. Not only that, but he had resigned from his job and had moved to the home town of his new wife. It did not take him long to realize that he had made another mistake and the couple parted. Frank began to think that he was being punished for the dissolution of his first marriage and the fact that he had deprived his son of a full-time father. He could not see that he was not listening to his own inner voice. He was rushing onto pathways that were not meant for him.

Frank returned to his home town, but unfortunately he had nowhere to live. His family could not accommodate him and he had lost contact with his friends. He had to find somewhere to live. He looked in the newspaper and scanned the 'To let' columns, but the rents were far beyond his means, especially as he did not have a job and was presently receiving benefits. Then he spied a column advertising bed and breakfast accommodation. Although he rather recoiled at the thought, he had no choice. He picked up the telephone and made an arrangement to view a room that very afternoon.

When Frank arrived at the house the door was opened by a young woman of similar age to himself who introduced herself as Janet. She showed him the accommodation offered and he was pleasantly surprised by the cleanliness and open, friendly atmosphere of the house. There were a couple of other men in residence, but the house was run by Janet, who owned it.

Frank decided that he would take the room, but there was one problem. He had not received his benefit money and could not pay the deposit required or the week's rent in advance. When he informed Janet of this fact, she laughed and told him, 'I'll trust you! You can move in straightaway if you want to.'

Frank could not describe how relieved he felt. If it had not been for Janet's kindness he would have had to sleep rough.

As the months passed by Frank realized that he was growing very fond of Janet. They had spent many long hours chatting to each another over cups of coffee and he felt that he knew her very well. She had told him about her own background and her disastrous marriage and Frank knew that they had great empathy with one another because of their similar backgrounds.

Gradually their friendship moved on to something deeper and they both realized that they cared for each other very much. Frank was determined not to make any more mistakes, but this time he was sure that Janet was the right person for him. She had shown him infinite kindness at the lowest point in his life when in reality she did not have to, as she did not know him.

The years passed and eventually Frank and Janet married. Frank found himself a job and became well established in his work. He was determined, however, to do better. With hard work and determination he eventually achieved far more than he ever thought possible. He and his wife had a comfortable lifestyle – a far cry from those earlier harsh years. Frank knew that he had at last found the person who was meant to share his life with him. He knew that at long last he was on the correct pathway and that the spirit people had allowed him, through his hard work and endeavour, to repay Janet the kindness she had shown him those years ago. He had been able to take her away from the life she was leading when he first met her – a life that involved very long hours and hard physical work. The people in the world of spirit had made sure that she was rewarded for caring for one of their beloved sons. After all, one good deed deserves another!

Jenny too tells of the time when a kindness was repaid.

Jenny had attended a travel trade promotion. She had gone on her own, but a couple of other girls had asked her to join them. Jenny had been very relieved, as she preferred not to attend these functions alone. To add to her difficulties, she had forgotten her spectacles and so needed somebody to help her with the paperwork involved. The three girls chatted and enjoyed each other's company before the promotion began. At the end, the compere asked everyone to look under their seats. Under the seat of one of Jenny's new friends was an envelope containing flight tickets to a part of the world she would never have ordinarily been able to afford to travel to. Jenny was pleased that one of her new friends had been rewarded for her kindness.

When the evening drew to a close Jenny wandered down to the station to catch the train home. As she walked past a shop doorway she caught sight of a man huddled up in an old army coat begging. As their eyes met she realized how lucky she was. She was on her way home to a warm bed in a warm house and a loving family, whereas this person had nothing but a dark damp doorway for the night. Without hesitation Jenny handed him some food that she had bought for her journey home on the train. She was rewarded with a bow of the head.

Jenny told me, 'I have never felt so humbled in my life. This was a beautiful soul in human form before my very eyes. His beautiful brown skin and deep brown eyes were like nothing I had ever seen on this Earth and I was certain I had seen an angel.'

As Jenny walked away she glanced behind her. The man had disappeared. Jenny feels that she had not met a human being but had experienced a test of her selflessness.

Two months later the telephone rang in Jenny's office. The person on the other end asked if she remembered putting her card into a prize draw on the evening of the promotion. Jenny did not remember doing this and was amazed to be told that she had won a brand new car. She was especially pleased as her old car was on its last legs and she needed a reliable car for her job.

Jenny firmly believes that the angel provided her with a new car as he knew that she needed it. She was being rewarded for her generosity that night. She says that her encounter with an angel will stay with her forever.

CHAPTER 24

Forgiveness

One of the more common themes of the letters I receive is that of forgiveness. People often ask whether their loved ones who have passed on to the world of spirit can forgive them for letting them down in some way. They may not have been around at the time of a loved one's physical death and been unable to say goodbye, or they may have had an argument with someone prior to their passing and not had the opportunity to rekindle the relationship before the physical death of that person.

I have mentioned in a previous chapter that just prior to his passing to the world of spirit my own father begged the forgiveness of his father because he had been unable to get back home to attend his funeral. I receive many letters from people who have been in a similar situation and I would say the same to them as I would have said to my father had I been given the opportunity. When we pass on from this physical world we are still aware of what is going on in the hearts and minds of the people we have left behind. My grandfather would have known just how upset my father was and would have been sorry to see him burdening himself with unnecessary guilt. He would have been aware that my father's duty was to care for his family and would not have wished Dad to use money that he could not afford to pay for an airfare merely to see his mortal remains interred. In his view, no forgiveness was necessary.

To all the people who are worrying that they in some way require forgiveness from a person in the spirit world I would say one thing and that is to forgive yourselves. When a person passes from their physical life to the heavenly state they become aware – aware of what is going on in our hearts and minds, aware of our emotions. They are aware that we may feel that we should have been at the bedside of a loved one at the time of passing, but they are also aware that sometimes that is not possible. They are aware of the feelings of the person who is experiencing enormous pangs of guilt because they did not mend an argument before the time of passing. They are also aware that all this guilt is entirely unnecessary. People in the world of spirit do not, in these circumstances, carry over resentments. If there has been an argument between two friends or family members and one of those friends or family members unfortunately departs their physical life before the relationship can be mended, they do not go on to the world of spirit carrying that emotion with them. No forgiveness is necessary.

Jean's story is a sad one in that she carried around a feeling of guilt for many months before speaking to me about it.

Jean and her mother Ada had always been very, very close. They were more like friends than mother and daughter. Although Jean was married and had two children of her own, she always made time each day to drop in to visit her mother, as she was now on her own. Jean's father had passed on to the spirit world four years earlier.

As the years passed and Ada grew older, they both dreaded the inevitable time when they would be parted. 'Promise me you'll be with me!' Ada used to say to Jean. 'I don't want to leave this life on my own. I want you to be there when I go!' Although the thought of losing her mother horrified Jean, she readily promised that when the time came she would certainly be there by her side.

When Ada was 84 years of age she had a stroke. It was not a severe one, but it was enough to keep her in hospital for a few days. Afterwards it was planned that she would at long last give up her independence and go to live with Jean and her husband. 'You'll be back home in no time,' the doctors told her.

The night before Ada was due to leave hospital she suffered a major heart attack. At 11 o'clock in the evening Jean received an urgent telephone call from the hospital telling her to get to there as quickly as she could because her mother would not survive the night.

Jean jumped into her car and drove the short distance to the hospital as quickly as she possibly could, but when she arrived she was told that her mother had passed from her physical life just minutes before. Jean was heartbroken. Not only did she feel as though she had lost her mother forever, but she also felt that she had let her down badly because she had not been able to keep her promise.

Jean got through Ada's funeral with difficulty and weeks later she was still feeling desperately sad and desperately guilty. She sought the advice of a bereavement counsellor, which helped her enormously in dealing with her loss, but she could not shake off the terrible feeling of guilt at having let her mother down.

Almost a year later I was introduced to Jean by somebody who thought I might be able to help her by explaining the system when a person passes over to the world of spirit. As I opened myself to her vibrations, the very first person to step forward was a short elderly lady.

'I'm Ada,' she announced, 'and I'm her mother.' She pointed towards Jean. 'Tell her to stop all this silly worrying! It wasn't her fault. I know she would have been with me if she could have been, but it wasn't meant to be. My family came for me and I had to go.'

I told Jean that I had her mother with me and passed on her words. 'Tell Jeannie that I'll always love her and watch over her and the kids,' Ada said, 'but she must get on with life. She must stop doing what she's doing to herself. I understand. We all do! We make these silly promises to one another when we're alive on the Earth, but who knows what's going to happen? All I want is for my lovely girl to be happy!'

A look of relief passed over Jean's face. 'I know it's my mother speaking,' she told me, 'because she's the only person who would ever dare call me "Jeannie".' She laughed. 'I feel so much better now, knowing that my mum knew that I didn't mean to let her down and that I did my best to get to her.'

Jean left my company that day feeling as though a huge burden had been lifted from her shoulders. She now knew that there was no need for forgiveness – her mother had confirmed that to her – and she now felt at peace.

CHAPTER 25

Saved by an Angel

I have received numerous stories from people who are convinced that they have been saved from certain physical death by their guardian angel. Even my wife Gwen has a story to tell from the days when she and her younger brother Alan were ignoring the advice of their parents one wintry afternoon.

At the time Gwen was about nine years of age, her brother would have been three years of age and they lived on a farm just outside Liverpool together with their mother and father and older sister. At the weekends Gwen and Alan used to wander out and play together. They used to climb trees and make dens and get up to all the usual things that young children do.

One particular winter weekend Gwen and Alan decided to go to a copse of trees quite close to the farmhouse. They had been told to keep well away from this area because in the middle of the trees there was quite a deep pond. Like most children, however, they decided that they would not pay any attention to what they had been told and they wandered over to see whether ice had formed on the pond.

Sure enough, it was covered with a thick layer of ice. Delighted, Gwen and Alan both picked up long branches that had fallen from the trees and started to smash the ice up. Unfortunately at one point Alan hit it with such gusto that the effort propelled him head first into the water.

Gwen panicked. She rushed to where Alan had fallen in and, holding on to a tree branch that was overhanging the pond, leaned as far as she could in an effort to try and catch hold of Alan. This met with no success. Next Gwen grabbed hold of a long sturdy branch that was lying on the ground and screamed to Alan to catch hold of it as she leaned out over the pond towards him. Fortunately he was able to grab the end of the branch and was pulled towards the edge of the pond.

Just at that moment their father came running up. He had heard Gwen screaming to Alan. He picked his small son up and ran towards the farmhouse, where Alan was immediately stripped of his clothing and plunged into a warm bath. An incident that could have had a horrible outcome had ended well. 'And Alan didn't even catch a cold!' Gwen's mother used to tell me when she related this story to me.

When reflecting on this incident Gwen has often told me that she knew that it wasn't her strength that had pulled Alan from the watery depths of the pond that day. 'I was only nine and I wasn't heavily built at all,' she will say. 'It was impossible for me to do what I did. That day I know that somebody was there helping me. I can still remember the feeling when I was pulling Alan towards the edge of the pond – it was as though somebody was there pulling with me. Don't forget that Alan was quite a well-built boy for his age, added to which he had on heavy clothing that was soaked with water. *And* it was so cold that we could hardly grip the branch of the tree. Somebody was definitely there! Somebody was looking over us!'

There is definitely a 'draw' where water and children are concerned, especially, it seems, during the cold winter months.

One winter's day when Mary was around 10 years of age she and her sister and one of her brothers decided to go and play on the golf course near to their house. It was a very cold day. The three children walked over the fairways and wandered down to a frozen pond which was located around 100 yards from the main road. There was no one around.

The children walked around the pond discussing who was going to be brave enough to try out the icy covering to see whether it would take their weight. Mary decided that she would try first and stepped out onto the ice. After she had gone a few feet, though, there was an ominous cracking sound, the ice gave way and she sank into the freezing water. Her sister tried to reach her, but as she edged out over the ice it began to crack beneath her weight and she was forced to jump back onto the bank. She yelled to Mary to swim, but Mary couldn't swim and began to panic.

Looking back at the bank, Mary saw her sister desperately trying to throw a float out in her direction. The next thing she knew, a float had landed next to her in the water. She grabbed hold of it and looked up to see a young man on the other end of it. He began to reel her in like a fish. He pulled her out of the water, put both his hands on her shoulders and asked if she was alright. Mary remembers that he had curly brown hair, wore glasses and was dressed in denims and a T-shirt. 'But it was his smile that I remember the most – it was the most reassuring and calming smile that I have ever seen on a person,' she reports.

Mary's sister meanwhile had been running around the pond. As she reached Mary and the stranger she stopped short. He told the children that they should go home. They all nodded and the stranger started to walk away up the fairway of the golf course. As he did so, he turned and smiled once more. It was then that the thought passed through Mary's mind that he must have been very cold indeed in just his light clothes.

The children started off for home but had gone no more than about 10 steps when they turned around to look behind them once more. The young man was nowhere in sight. Mary says that there was no way that he could have walked across the fairway in just those few seconds. She asked her sister and brother whether they had noticed where he had gone. They were both as puzzled as Mary at the sudden disappearance of her saviour. The only footsteps on the frosty grass leading away from the pond were those of the three children.

Then Mary asked her sister where the man had come from, but she replied that she didn't know. She said he had suddenly appeared as Mary was disappearing under water for a third time and had grabbed the float and pulled her out. 'But he pulled me out on the side of the pond opposite to where you were,' Mary exclaimed. At that, all the children fell silent.

To this day Mary is convinced that the young man was her guardian angel and that he had come to save her from a watery grave.

CHAPTER 26

Signs from the Spirit People

My own experience of signs and signals from people in the spirit world are innumerable. Almost every day of my life something happens to make me aware that there is a spirit person around just letting me know that they are there without wishing to intrude upon my consciousness by attempting to communicate either clairvoyantly or clairaudiently.

The signs are mostly small but significant. They could be the aroma of perfume or tobacco, the small movement of curtains where there is no draught, something being inexplicably moved away from its rightful place or the glimpse of a shadow out of the corner of my eye. The most significant signals are the ones I receive from my spirit guide Sam. He lets me know he is around by rapping on the television set whilst I am sitting back relaxing and watching a favourite programme. A thought may be filtering into my mind or I may be thinking of something relevant to a lost loved one. I may even have a problem that is vexing me. Sam always makes a rapping sound to let me know that I am not alone and that he is there with me.

Even our animals notice when there is a spirit presence. Penny, the German Shepherd, will prick her ears and look alert as her eyes follow a spirit visitor across the room. Jack, our standard poodle, will peer under an occasional table wagging his tail frantically at the spirit return of Jasper, one of our cats of whom he was particularly fond and who used to frequently curl up under that self-same table. By the reactions of our pet animals Gwen always knows when a person or a pet has returned in visitation.

On the day of my beloved mother-in-law's funeral, the fingers on a wall clock stopped at the precise time of the commencement of the funeral service – a sure sign that Joanie was around and thinking of us just as much as we were thinking of her.

I write a weekly column for a local newspaper and a popular weekly magazine. In this column I answer questions sent to me by readers. A fair percentage of the letters

I receive relate to the movement of items in a home or the smell of cigarettes or tobacco in a house where nobody smokes, the familiar aroma of the favourite perfume of a lost loved one or maybe even the smell of baking cakes when no cooking is taking place. These are all signs used by loved ones in spirit to let us know that they are around.

Gwen's father loved gardening in his later years. He especially loved roses. During the summer, when roses are picked from our garden, you will often see the flowers move after they have been placed into a vase. On the anniversary of his death in the month of October, the fronds of a house plant will often wave around. It is as though he is waving goodbye once again but reminding us that we will be reunited once again in the future.

I am notorious for misplacing items such as door or car keys, cufflinks and other small objects. I just cannot remember where I have put them. Gwen, however, is far more organized – I suppose because she has to be! But if she says that she has put something down somewhere you can guarantee that that is where it will be. Sometimes, though, Gwen will be searching for something and will say, 'But I know where I put it – just there!' An exhaustive search in all likely places will not bring the item to light – until, that is, we return to the original place where Gwen left it. There it will be, looking as though it has never moved. On other occasions Gwen will be adamant that she has left something in a particular place only for it to resurface some time later in an entirely different room.

Of course Gwen is not the only person who finds items moving to another location or disappearing completely. These are the workings of spirit to draw our attention to them. We may not be listening to them or reading the signs as we should. It is difficult for people in the spirit world to convey messages to those who have no mediumistic abilities and sometimes they have to rely on plain logic to click in.

Generally, though, the signs from people in the spirit world are just to let us know that they are around us in visitation. They are just calling in to say hello and, like people who visit us in the physical world, they like us to know they are there.

Pauline's grandmother always used to let her granddaughter know when she was around at times when cooking or baking was underway. Pauline could always be sure that just as she was about to remove something hot from the oven, the oven gloves would either fall on the floor or swing on the hook where they were kept. This was a sign from her grandmother to remind Pauline to put them on.

The significance of this was that Pauline's grandmother had received a horrific burn to her hand and arm one day whilst she was removing a dish of stewed meat from the oven. When she was still in her physical life she would always remind Pauline to protect her hands when taking items out of the oven and she has not changed one iota since passing over to the world of spirit.

Zelma's husband has passed to the spirit world, but he never ever forgets their wedding anniversary. As the date in June comes around each year, Zelma knows that the musical box on her dressing table, a gift from her husband many years ago, will begin to tinkle.

'It's as though he's telling me that he hasn't forgotten, so I'd better remember too,' she laughs. 'He was a bit of a stickler like that! I have to admit that I was the one who used to forget! He's making sure that I don't do that anymore, even though he's gone.'

There are so many ways in which our loved ones in spirit let us know that they are around. Some signs are definite and precise, as in the case of Pauline and Zelma. Others are more subtle. However, they are all made just to let us know that we're not forgotten by our loved ones in spirit any more than they are forgotten by the ones they left behind.

Rhona called me during the time that I had an office in Liverpool city centre. She was most upset. She had lost her mother Violet to the world of spirit almost 10 years earlier. A framed photograph of her standing in the garden with Rhona's son Gary had hung on the wall in the lounge all that time, undisturbed apart from when it had been taken down for decorating purposes. Gary had grown up and was now a young man. He had joined the army and was at that time on a tour of duty in Northern Ireland.

The night previous to Rhona's telephone call to me, the photograph had inexplicably fallen from the wall. Rhona's husband had examined the picture hook and the cord from which the frame was suspended and could find nothing wrong with them – the cord was still intact, the picture hook unbent and still firmly embedded in the wall.

'Do you think it's a sign that something's going to happen to Gary?' Rhona asked me. 'Is he going to die?'

I quickly opened myself up to the spirit world, hoping that Violet or another member of Rhona's family would deem it fit to communicate with me. 'Hold on! Hold on, Rhona!' I told her, 'I think I'm getting something!'

As I sat there willing somebody to step forward, I thankfully heard Sam's voice quietly in the background. 'Tell Rhona not to worry,' he said. 'All will be well. Gary will return home to his mother.'

There was nothing more, but at least I could reassure Rhona that her son would be returned to her and was not in fact due to pass on to the world of spirit.

'Oh, thank goodness!' Rhona exclaimed. 'I just could not bear to lose my son. It was bad enough when my mother passed away, but to lose my son would just about kill me too!'

The following day I received another telephone call from Rhona. 'It *was* a sign from my mother,' she told me. 'I heard today that Gary has been slightly injured during a skirmish on the streets in Belfast, but that he is safe and will be sent home within the next three or four days. Thank Sam for not telling me that he had been hurt but for just reassuring me that he would come home. I know that I would have been worried sick.'

I put the telephone down. I was so pleased that Gary was going to be fine and would be home soon and I had to agree with Rhona that Violet had been giving her a sign that although there was going to be a slight mishap involving Gary, he would not be badly harmed – just as the photograph hanging on the wall had slipped and fallen but not been harmed!

Derek Acorah's Ghost Towns
From the hit TV series

The companion book to LIVINGtv's hit series, *Derek Acorah's Ghost Towns* will answer all your questions about ghostly encounters. *Ghost Towns* sees Derek take to the road to meet the people of Britain, knocking on the doors of unsuspecting members of the public to deliver psychic messages. In each of the towns visited across the UK, Derek and the team face a host of fresh challenges, unearthing strange stories that have plagued the local residents for years.

- In **Maidstone**, are the brothers of the Feng Shui Restaurant being haunted or guided by their ancestors?
- In **Royston,** who is the drunken spirit who haunts an old police station?
- In **Faversham**, what happens when Derek channels the spirit of a dying man in the Brewery?
- Will Derek's Doorstep Divinations always be welcome?
- Can Derek convince even the most hardened sceptics?

'Britain's best-known medium.' *Daily Express*